WRITE

TO

KILL

ABOUT THE AUTHOR

David P Perlmutter lives in London, England. He is the very proud father of four children and has two grandsons.

It was while living in Portugal several years ago, that David started to write his first book, **Wrong Place Wrong Time** as a blog, but a friend, and then editor, who read the first couple of chapters, told him it was too good for a blog, it must be a book. Since then this book has become a #1 BESTSELLER on Amazon with over a thousand 5* reviews and has been traditionally published. It is also now in development to be made into a movie, backed by a powerful production team in the shape of Golden Mile Productions and No Reservations Entertainment, and including Bafta award-winning executive producer Mark Foligno, from films such as The King's Speech and Moon .

David's second book, **Five Weeks**, is another true story and catalogues a trip to America during which he was almost left for dead in a Pennsylvanian wood. His third book is called **24 Hours In New York** about his failed attempt to 'make it big' in America. David's fourth book is another true story, **13,** highlights four major events of his life when he turned 13.

Apart from writing, David spends a lot of time promoting and marketing authors across the world on his social media platforms. He has written eight books on marketing for the indie author in his **My Way** brand, which can also be found on Amazon and on his website.

David enjoys engaging with his 55,000 plus followers on Twitter @davepperlmutter and invites all his readers to join him there in 'conversation'.

DavidPPerlmutter

OTHER BOOKS BY DAVID P PERLMUTTER

TRUE STORIES

Wrong Place Wrong Time (Book to Movie)

Five Weeks

24 Hours In New York

13

CRIME FICTION

Write to Kill

Write to Survive

BOOK MARKETING

My Way Won

My Way Too

My Way Free – Trending on Twitter

My Way Four – May The 4th Be with You

My Way 5 – About Life

My Way 6 – Sex for The Beach

My Way - LinkedIn

My Way to Getting Published

CHAPTERS

Frankie Goes to Hollywood

West Hampstead

The Krays

Sky News

Breakfast TV

Kensington

Chelsea

Kings Road

Grieving Wife

Tower of London

Guilty Feelings

Glued Together

Tin of Weed

Eyes and Ears

Fifty Shades

HE'S PUTTING

THE DEAD

IN DEADLINE

MORON

EYEING the blurry headlights in the rear-view mirror, I caught my eye and glanced at the person staring back.

I didn't recognise myself.

Or what I imagined I was about to become.

As I drove on the M40, a shade after eleven on a miserable, wet Saturday evening in November, a number of cars, one straight up my backside, creating spray from the saturated tarmac, were flashing me to get out of their way, even though my right foot was pressed hard, flat out on the metal, hitting seventy. Which is an accomplishment for my ageing car, believe me.

The downpour that had been rhythmically drumming on my windscreen most of the journey, temporarily making driving treacherous, due to only one functioning windscreen wiper, had finally stopped lashing it down. Some moron, probably pissed after a night out a few days ago had completely ripped off the passenger side wiper when my car was parked close to the building where I live but luckily, if you can call it that, had left the driver's in place, otherwise I'd have been well and truly fucked and unable to go to my 'so called' business meeting tonight.

You may be thinking why on earth am I going to a meeting on a Saturday night, especially having left a warm bed with an exceptionally beautiful girl under the duvet, but this was not like any other meeting, I can assure you of that. There was no office, no board room, or even colleagues. It was going to be just the two of us, in a dilapidated warehouse, in a deserted place, in the middle of nowhere, on a day and at a time that suited him.

BLACK T-SHIRT

TAKING a long final pull of a cigarette until there was no more to smoke, I flicked the butt through the small gap I'd left open at the top of the window, out into the chill wet darkness. But as quick as the remaining ash hit the outside world, it flew back in and over my black T-shirt. Dusting the ash into my top rather than off it, I shifted from third to fourth gear.

The thought of what I'd agreed to do accelerated in my mind as I veered from the inside lane, over the other two and exited at junction two. Taking a narrow lane, a mile down the road, I lit another cigarette, the last of the pack, and threw the empty packet onto the passenger side floor, to join the many others that had made their home there.

This was my fifth in the hour since I'd left my flat, with an attractive brunette asleep in my bed. I really must give up these damn things. No, not the brunette, I'm not that stupid. Or am I? The fags. I've been saying that for months though, maybe a year, I just can't kill the habit, even though I know that one day, they could eventually kill me.

I was nervous. Very nervous. Why? Because in a few minutes, in the building that I was approaching, in this isolated area in Buckinghamshire, I would be meeting him.

DARKER SIDE

TURNING off the country lane in total darkness, with just my headlights as a guide, I took a right, then a left, which led into an uneven forecourt, full of potholes and puddles, and pulled up outside the deserted derelict building. How I managed to find this place from the directions I'd been given was a miracle, especially with only a half moon for light, and the fact that I don't have a sat nav as my car is it's an antique. It even has a cassette player, that's how ancient it is. But it does have electric windows and, my pride and joy, pop-up lights. Also, being stuck out in the countryside, I had no signal on my phone to get Google maps or any other map app. It was dark, with not a light in sight and as I checked the time on my mobile it beeped as I did so, indicating that I had only eight percent of juice left.

Why didn't I charge it before I left home?

Arriving ten minutes early, which is a feat for me, as people have said that I'll be late for my own funeral, *hopefully this won't be it,* I lit another cigarette, with the remains of the cigarette I was smoking. Keeping my headlights on full beam, I followed the stream of light that captured the deepening evening mist and hesitantly made my way inside the shell of the warehouse.

As I stepped in, with the luminosity of the moon my only light, I disturbed a kit of pigeons that were pecking at the soggy floor. They cocked their heads in my direction, their beady eyes staring at me, then flew off in different directions to the highest point of the roof, leaving their white and brown excrement all over the grey coloured concrete.

I trod carefully so as not to step into the mass of bird crap as I observed the vast vacant, fragmented construction, made of corrugated metal, with gaps in the roof giving the pigeons the freedom to fly in and out at their leisure. I checked my phone, now with just seven percent juice left and only five minutes to our meeting. Five minutes until he arrives. That's if he's punctual. Again, I began to wonder what the hell was I doing? *Why was I doing this? Why am I here?* I whispered those questions, out loud, to no one, but me, as I waited patiently but nervously in this tin hub of a desperate building.

These were the same questions that had been going over and over in my head since I'd left my flat, after making passionate love to that girl, Lisa, the petite, grass green-eyed brunette beneath the duvet, over an hour earlier.

That's why I didn't charge my phone.

The same girl who I'd been seeing for the past few months, which is the longest relationship I've been in for three years. All the others within that time, and there have been quite a few, only lasted the night. Lisa and I met at a friend of a friend's party in Clerkenwell. She's a nurse, seven years younger than me, lives in North West London, not far from me, a couple of miles or so, where she shares a flat with four friends, all colleagues at The Royal Free in Hampstead. She stays over at mine at the weekends and sometimes during the week. I assume so she can get away from talking shop twenty-four seven. We hit it off straight away, it was like fate really, unlike what I'm about to do, but she knows nothing of what I am getting myself into. She knows nothing of this darker side of me. Come to think of it, I knew nothing of this darker side of me. All she knows, is that I'm a struggling first-time author, and I mean struggling, not with writer's block, well maybe, but financially.

My bank account was way, way over its overdraft, in fact, it was on the brink of being frozen. The rent on my flat was four months late, and trust me, it isn't cheap. I hadn't paid a single utility bill for months or my council tax, and to top it all off, along with the bailiffs on my case, I had menacing loan sharks circling and banging on my door every other day, wanting to break my legs, unless I paid them what I owed, with huge interest. You see, my mountain of debt began when I lost my job as office manager for an estate agency six months ago, a month after I moved into this flat. They closed the branch without any warning at all and since then I've struggled to find another job. Believe me, I've tried. So, while I've been looking, I've been trying to fulfil a lifelong dream, which is to write a book and become a bestselling author. I've written a few short stories before but I've always wanted to write a novel.

But I was a long way off becoming a bestselling author and signing copies at Waterstones. Turns out that writing a bestselling novel is much harder than you might think. I'd written nothing, maybe a thousand words of nothing, that's all, then not another word, not even a letter. I have what author's call writer's block, like I said. I was way behind where I wanted to be with my first draft. My editor, well, I say my editor. My mate who has lived in London for a number of years, had some time ago emailed his mum, who lives in New York, a short story of mine. His mum, a semi-retired editor, who used to edit many books for a number of top USA Today bestselling authors, was so impressed with my writing and one of my short stories, that she encouraged me to write that first novel. I couldn't turn down this opportunity and thankfully last month, she agreed to be my editor, on the understanding that firstly, the book will be written within three months, as she has another project scheduled for the beginning of next year, *no pressure there then*, and secondly, I will pay her a fee once the book is published, and the royalties start to roll in.

Whenever that will be. If it ever happens.

She is very sweet, reminds me of my mum. God bless her.

So, every couple of days my editor sends me an email asking when the first couple of chapters will be available for editing. Every reply I return says the same thing. *In a few days.* But will I ever get this book finished or even properly started? Of course, it's my dream like I've said, but with my plummeting financial situation, not only did I need money to pay thousands to get people off my back, I needed money just to live day to day, and having none and pretending I had to Lisa, completely threw me from my writing.

My money worries played on my mind but I still don't know why I'd agreed to do what I'm about to do. Well I do. The dough. But I couldn't back out now, even if I wanted to, and believe me, I did. I'd given my word and he's not the kind of man you back down to. No way. Once you've given your word, you keep to your word. Or you'll face the consequences. And I didn't want to face mine.

You see, with him, once you've shaken hands, you've shaken hands.

Otherwise you won't have a hand to shake.

Get my drift.

SIX FEET UNDER

RIGHT on time. Shaking with dread and additionally shivering from the cold, damp evening, I watched with envy from inside the warehouse as his brand new, personalised plate, top of the range blacked-out Range Rover entered the forecourt, crunching the wet gravel as it did so.

Who said crime doesn't pay?

Splashes of water and grit sploshed up from under the tyres, spraying the wheel arch and front bumper, and as it did so, I took a step back, with fear at the very sight of him. The heavy rain that had poured down during the day and early evening had now subsided but had left plenty of evidence. My twenty-year-old rust bucket, my reliable Volkswagen Golf, with one wiper and maximum speed of seventy, that I'd parked a few feet away, just minutes earlier, looked like, David against his gleaming Goliath.

Finishing off another cigarette, from a new pack retrieved earlier from the glove compartment, I lit yet another while I waited for him, as the moisture diffused through the air of the abandoned unlit warehouse on the outskirts of this wealthy green belt area. The half-moon, along with the headlights of my car and his casting the only light through the roof and row of shattered windows to the front of the grey steel-framed building. The cold, damp, darkness of the interior, matched the exterior, except for the evening fog rolling in from the nearby countryside. It was a month before December and autumn had cemented itself, with winter around the corner. I loathed this time of year with the nights closing in, even as early as half four in the afternoon.

Give me the sun all year round, any day of the week.

Gasping on the cigarette like it was my last, my heart gathered pace as I heard his monster of a car come to a halt. I took a deep breath and another step back, nearly choking on the smoke that I'd just inhaled when I heard the slam of his car door. I was nervous. And I had a right to be. A mate of mine. Mate? He was no mate trust me, never has been and never will be. Anyway, Jake was a friend, of a friend, of another friend, who had introduced me to him.

Him. Him being Mad Dog Maddox, the person who at this very moment is walking towards this building, the very same building that I'm standing in, with his thundering footsteps hitting the gravel gaining momentum with every step.

Jake was a bit of an unsavoury character to say the least, always on the wrong side of the law, banged up more times than I've had hot dinners and not my normal hangout guy at all, but he knew the situation I was in, as in, I needed money, and quick, and he knew how to make a fast buck, so he had arranged a meet. The three of us met last week in an out-of-the-way café in West London for the first time, and I'd been given instructions on what to do. I'd heard a lot about Mad Dog, his underhand business dealings and personal antics from Jake, but I'd never met him on a one-to-one basis, only the once last week, never mind in a vacant warehouse in the middle of nowhere, in the middle of the night, alone, like tonight. Like now, with no one else knowing where I am, apart from Mad Dog. I still don't know why I agreed to do this. Well. I do. Like I said, the cash. You know, money talks.

And the cash was screaming at me.

Crashing my second cigarette in as many minutes under the sole of my black laced shoe, into the moist concrete floor, a hulk of a man appeared, stooping his menacing six-foot three frame as he entered the remains of the building through what was once a doorway. A trail of water escaped from the surround above him as he did so, and he let out a growl as he wiped away the liquid from his bald head with the palm of his right hand. Even when he was hunched, he still looked towering and threatening. There was me, five-foot eleven and not at all what you would call stocky, his presence made me feel overwhelmingly intimated, the majority of people I know would have felt the same.

Standing not more than ten feet away from me, sucking on a cigar that he'd just lit, with the flame momentarily brightening up the dull surroundings, his eyes darted around the empty warehouse, as he shook his head in revulsion at the state of the dilapidated building he'd chosen to meet in. He then turned to me, his mouth twitching at the corners. His disconcerting eyes burning into mine.

"You ready for tomorrow, like we discussed?" he said in a hard-hitting Cockney, East End London grunt.

What, no hello or how are you?

"Yes, Mr Maddox. I think I'm ready, yes, yes, I'm ready," I replied nervously.

"You sure, because you don't sound it?"

"Yes, I'm sure. Totally, I'm sure."

But I was far from fucking sure.

"You know why I'm giving you this job to do?"

"Because you know I need the money?"

"No. Well, I know you need the money, but it's more than that, it's because you're clean."

"What do you mean, clean?"

"You've answered your own question pal."

"How's that?"

"Jesus. You are a fucking virgin. You're clean, because this is your first time."

"Of course it is. I've never done anything like this before. Never been in trouble with the police, never been arrested. Not even a fine."

"Exactly. Invisible to them."

"I see."

"This is what I wanted. I knew from the meeting last week that you were the guy for the job. No police record. No arrests. Not on their radar. Get me now?"

"Yes, I do. Not known to the police."

"Precisely. So, you know where you're going, you know exactly what he looks like from the photo I showed you, where he'll be and where he lives?"

"Yes, I remember what he looks like, and I still have the details you gave me when we met last week," I answered.

"What do you mean, still?"

"The details, you gave me."

"What the piece of paper?"

"Yes." *Fuck, why did I say that.*

"For fuck's sake. Have you got that on you now?"

"Yes," I answered hesitantly.

"Then fucking give it to me. Now," he demanded.

I pulled the note from the front pocket of my jeans. He reached out his right arm towards me and as I held the paper, his huge hand gripped mine as he stared at me, his eyes digging into mine, deliberately blowing pungent cigar smoke in my direction.

I swear I could hear the echo of my heartbeat bounce off the corrugated walls.

Then he spoke, as he released my hand.

"This can't happen. This is your first fucking mistake. Do not leave any fucking evidence around. I mean it. If I get traced to this, you'll be gone without a trace, understand or do….." he didn't need to say another threating word, his sinister glare told me everything I needed to know.

"I won't fuck up again, I swear. I won't," I butted in, signalling with my hands.

"You'd better not. I've been here two minutes and you've already fucked up."

"I won't, I swear."

"You've got the address in your head, yes?"

"Yes."

"Are you sure?"

"Yes."

"Good."

As he replied, he lit the piece of paper, with the end of his cigar. I watched it disintegrate as it fell from his huge right hand to the ground.

"Because pal, you don't want to end up like this, do you, do you now?" he teased with a grin.

"No, not at all Mr Maddox," I replied trying hard to retain what little composure I had left, if I'd ever had any at all on this particular evening.

"So, you know exactly where you're going and what you've got to do?"

"Exactly, yes, so don't worry."

He laughed. Out loud.

"Don't worry. Jesus Christ. You tell me to not to worry. I've taken a chance on you. You've already fucked up and I do worry. Why, because this is your first time and you can't let me down. I've hired you because I know you need the wedge, but you can't screw up. You just can't. And remember, I'm paying you a lot of fucking money. Understand?"

If I wasn't nervous before, which I was, I truly was now.

"Yes. Sorry, yes. Of course, I understand. I will not let you down. I swear, I will not let you down," I repeated with a slight stutter. Even though I've never stuttered in my life before.

"Good. Just making it clear. Talking of which."

He reached into the inside pocket of his immaculate camel hair coat, and even though it was a chilly night, a bead of sweat escaped from my forehead and I felt it run down the side of my face. I had flashes of him pulling something else out of his pocket, you know, like a gun or some sort of weapon, but thankfully it was just an envelope.

Between you and me, Jake had told me that Mad Dog had a reputation of having a very unpredictable personality, which kept me on edge. Trust me. One minute he could be on the verge of whacking me, the next he's my best mate.

Hence the nickname Mad Dog.

"Half now and exactly the same amount at the wake, not the funeral, which you can't attend, the police will be there for sure. Once his body is six feet under your job will be done. Right. Okay."

It wasn't a question. It was a statement. And I wasn't about to cross-examine him, no chance. I nodded and smiled within as he tossed the cash filled envelope towards me. I gathered it up and without opening or counting the money I stuffed it inside my favourite leather jacket, which was as old as my car sitting out in the forecourt. Jake had warned me not to open or count the cash in his presence, as the last person who'd attempted to do so, had had his fingers broken there and then. That, in his eyes, was showing total disrespect. And, believe me, for some reason at that moment, I had respect for him, even though I knew others didn't. But, as I said, they got their bones broken and I wanted to drive back home with all my fingers intact, safely and painlessly gripping the steering wheel.

"One more thing."

I looked up and rolled my eyes in my mind.

As you do. I just wanted to get out of there as quick as possible.

17

"Once you have done it, you let her know, you let my daughter know straight away and tell her exactly where he is, tell her where the fucker is bleeding to death, okay?"

"Okay, sure, but I don't have her number, I don't even know her name."

"Didn't he tell you?"

"No, he didn't." I thought of Jake.

"Fucking muppet," Mad Dog replied out loud.

He took another drag of his cigar, as a momentary break of deadly silence surrounded us.

"Come here," he demanded.

I walked nervously towards him, pigeon steps, and as I did, one flew above.

"Give me your hand."

He pulled a pen out from the inside of his jacket, as I rubbed the sweat from my palm onto my jeans. He grabbed my hand and wrote her name and number on my palm.

"Don't wash your hands before you've memorised the number."

I nodded, then took a few steps back, and didn't say a word. I didn't want to open my useless mouth for fear of unleashing his wrath again.

"You really sure you're up for this? I can't afford any mistakes!" he said taking a step towards me, with a menacing stare.

"Yes, yes, I am, I'll deal with it Mr Maddox," I replied, trying to sound tough, like a pro, taking a step back.

"Good. You'd better had for the sake of my business and family, they mean a lot to me."

Ah, business comes first.

He stared at me with a lingering glare. His menacing eyes locked on mine, which made me even more anxious as he puffed away on the receding cigar **and blew out smoke into my direction.**

"I don't give a fuck how you do it, just fucking do it and finish the bastard off."

Just then, I thought again about what I'd got myself involved in. I was completely out of my depth, completely, but my need of the dollar had pulled me in, fast and headfirst.

"Another thing."

What now.

He produced another brown envelope and pulled out a small mobile phone.

"This is for you, think of it as a, you know, sort of company phone. You need to charge it. The charger's in here. We'll communicate by this phone only. It's untraceable. No one, not even the Old Bill can trace this beauty, so don't give this number to anyone. No family, friends, no one. Understand?"

"Yes of course. I understand."

"I mean it. No girlfriend, boyfriend, fucking no one, alright."

"Yep, no one. Honest."

"Good. I like honesty."

Yeah, of course you do.

"Also, once you've done the deed, take a photo. I want to see him dead. I want to see that bastard dead."

Swallowing, I replied. "Sorry, you want me to take a photo of him dead, and send it to you?"

"That's what I said. Fucking dead. You got a problem with that?"

"No. No, not all at."

"Good, I thought not, also, keep his phone. I want it."

"You want me to keep his phone?"

"That's what I said. Are you listening?"

"Yes. Yes I am."

"There could be useful information on there for me."

"Okay, sure."

"And be sure to turn it off."

"Okay."

"Oh, one more thing."

Jesus, he's worse than Colombo.

"I'll let you know when the wake takes place."

Then, without saying another word, he turned his back on me, stooped under the arch of the doorway, swaying away from the dripping water and walked over to his car, with cigar smoke trailing and eventually evaporating behind him. Staying inside until I heard his engine spark to life, I lit another cigarette. I know I should give up these bad boys, or at least cut down. One day maybe, but not now. I can't do it now.

Hearing him rev up his four-by-four, water splashed in all directions as he drove his beast out of the parking area with ripples circulating the shallow potholes. As I walked to my battered beauty, I flicked the cancer stick into one of the puddles and watched the flame sizzle to nothing. I climbed in, strapped myself safe, wrote her number down on a packet of cigarettes, lit up another and began to drive the forty odd miles back to London with nothing but tomorrow night on my mind.

WRONG PLACE WRONG TIME

AFTER parking my car, and just before one a.m., I entered the mansion block, the place I called home, on West End Lane in West Hampstead and closed the Georgian style main front door behind me. I ambled upstairs to the second floor trying not to trip over the threads of the carpet that were hanging loose on every other step. Judging by the stained, threadbare old-fashioned mishmash flowery pattern, I assumed the carpet hadn't been replaced, or even cleaned in years and I'm paying top dollar for this place. I guess that's London prices for you. Having opened the door to my one bedroom flat, which was one of two on this floor, I popped my head round the bedroom door and spotted Lisa asleep, with her nurse's uniform crumpled on the floor beside the bed.

She looked so peaceful, totally oblivious of my whereabouts tonight and what's in store tomorrow for that matter. Leaving her to sleep, as I knew she had to get up early for another twelve-hour shift, I went into the partially fitted kitchen, which was just about big enough to fit a small table in the centre and pulled a bottle of beer from the fridge. The bottle looked so lonely standing on its own, apart from a carton of semi-skimmed milk on the shelf above keeping it company, ready for tomorrow morning's coffee, which as always would be very much needed, actually essential in order to get me jump-started for the day ahead. I hooked the lid off the beer and sank four gulps, one after the other as my throat felt as harsh as the words Mad Dog had said to me earlier.

I don't give a fuck how you do it, just fucking do it and finish the bastard off.

At that point I wondered what the poor sod had done to deserve the fate which lay in store for him, but as I took off my jacket, placed it on the back of the wooden chair, removed the envelope and sat down, any sympathy for my intended murder victim disappeared. I ripped the seal, tipped the envelope, and a pile of crisp, brand new fifty-pound notes, and I mean a pile, and I mean crisp, fell onto the cream cotton tablecloth that had been given to me by one of my aunts as a moving in present. *Only an aunt would buy a single guy a tablecloth.* I stared at the heap of notes as I sat back in the chair and exhaled. I knew what I was doing was wrong, so wrong on so many levels, but the cash in front of me looked sexy and seductive, and there and then, I swear I got a fucking hard on just looking at it.

But, I was now in right over my head. It was him or me, and I didn't want it to be me. I leaned forward, flicked the first rubber band off one of the clusters and started to count the mass of notes. I hadn't known the exact amount I would be paid, but I knew it would be more money that I've ever seen or handled in years. I counted a thousand pounds within twenty seconds, but that wasn't it. By the end of three minutes, forty-five seconds, I had counted ten thousand pounds. TEN THOUSAND fucking POUNDS. More money than I'd seen in ten years in one lump sum, in front of me, in cash, sitting on a one ninety-nine tablecloth. I knew that, as the price tag was still hanging from it. It's the thought that counts. That's what my beautiful dear old mum always taught me, bless her soul.

It doesn't matter how much it cost, it's the thought that counts. Only if she saw me now, what would be her thoughts? I felt a stab of shame as her face flashed before me. She would be horrified, completely devastated, that her only child was about to commit such an evil act as murdering someone for money.

But I had no choice.

I banished her from my thoughts as my attention once again was pulled by the tantalising sight of the cash in front of me. But this was only a down-payment. I'd be getting another ten once I'd finished the job.

I downed another swig of beer, lit another cigarette, sat back and blew out perfect smoke rings as I stared at the cash before me. The circular clock fixed to the wall opposite, with its long and short hands smiling at me, indicated it was ten to two. I badly needed to get some shut eye, but I was far too hyped to lay still and anyway, I didn't want to disturb Lisa.

24

I poured myself the final remains of the whisky Lisa had given me two weeks ago, along with two hundred packets of cigarettes, after her weekend in Spain. One of her flatmates was getting hitched and had had her hen weekend in Barcelona, *a place I haven't visited.* Believe me, those fags and the one litre bottle of Destilerias Y Crianza had come into my life at exactly the right time.

Thoughts of how I would get away with murder tomorrow night swirled around my head, just like the whisky in the tumbler I was holding. How would I do it? And what will happen if I got caught by the police, I'll be banged up for life. I've never been in trouble with the Old Bill. Never had a criminal record. Never been arrested. Never been fined, never mind murdering someone. I'd even been nervous about getting pulled over for having one wiper on the car. What was I thinking? More to the point, was I thinking? Also, what would I use? I didn't want to use a gun. I haven't got a gun, I've never used a gun, and where the fuck would I get a gun from anyway?

With my mind ticking over, I clocked the set of knives sitting on the Formica worktop next to the microwave. I took a swig of whisky from the tumbler, stood up and walked over to the five-piece knife set. Each one of them with a different coloured handle and matching blade. I pulled them out one at a time, pricking the palm of my hand with the tip of each blade feeling the sharpness and looking at them like I was some sort of pro. I picked out the biggest knife, the green one, the colour of a Granny Smith's apple, with the widest blade, and juggled it from one hand to the other, like a piece of fruit.

Lifting my black T-shirt, I began to jab the tip gently against my stomach, tapping the blade against my skin, feeling the sharpness of the tip. I took another sip of whisky to dull the pain as I jabbed harder and quicker, until I felt a tear. I looked down and noticed a piercing of the skin. A warm trickle of blood escaped and rolled onto my brown leather belt. I pulled the knife to eye level and spotted a speck of red on the tip. I'll admit, it did cause some discomfort. I thought of my victim, this was nothing. I couldn't imagine the pain he was going to be feeling.

Gaping at the weapon in my hand with my blood on its tip, I knew I couldn't use it as the set had been a gift from Lisa, it just seemed wrong, not that anything I was about to do was right. **Can you imagine if she found out that I've murdered someone with the knives she kindly bought me? She'll kill me. Also, if I killed someone with a knife she bought, would that make her an accessory to murder?**

That was it though, it had to be a knife. But the last time I'd used a knife, these knifes, was when I was slicing onions, vegetables and chicken for the romantic meal I'd made for us both the other night, and tomorrow I'd being cutting another type of meat. As I envisaged the act I had to commit, a chill played tag along my spine, like someone just stepped over my grave.

By now it was approaching three in the morning and the notion of how I would murder someone made me dead tired, so I stabbed the cigarette out in the overflowing ashtray, finished off the malt, wrapped a rubber band around each bundle of cash and stuffed them back into the envelope.

As I rolled into bed naked, apart from a plaster running across my self-inflicted wound, trying not to wake sleeping beauty beside me, I carefully slid the envelope into the bedside table drawer, hiding it beneath the book I was reading, Wrong Place Wrong Time, a gritty true story, which I could really relate to. I placed my mobile on top of the bedside table and the new company mobile charging under the bed, knowing that one of the messages I'd be sending tomorrow, would be an image of a dead body.

OLYMPIC HURDLER

RUNNING along a West London street, with heavy rain pelting down, I glanced back and kept on glancing back, but he kept running, he was running after me with a gun, pointed, straight at me. Fuck this has all gone horribly wrong. It wasn't meant to be like this. This was not the fucking plan. He was bleeding from his forearm where I'd stabbed him, but then, to my surprise and alarm, he'd pulled a gun out and my knife was in no way a defence against his weapon. Throwing the knife straight at him, barely causing any further injury, I'd taken off and was now running for my life, taking a right down a narrow road, just off High Street Ken.

As he ran after me, with the gun in his hand, I consecutively dragged over two or three wheelie bins as I ran past them, hoping he would take a tumble and fall, but he vaulted over them like a fucking Olympic hurdler and kept on running. Skidding on the slippery wet cobbles, I managed to keep my balance and swerved right into a narrow alley, then

28

took a sharp left into an even narrower alley which was overshadowed by high rise brick walls.

As my pace began to falter on the damp cobbled ground, I stood against a wall in the shadow of darkness, with the rain receding to a light fall. The sound of my beating heart bounced off the stone structure as I waited a minute, maybe two, but it seemed more like ten. I thought I'd lost him, I really did, but he spotted me and ran towards me pointing the gun in my direction.

Acting within a split second, bypassing him like a flash, like my life depended on it, which it did, I ran out of the alley and into a little side road with a row of two storey townhouses either side. The place was pitch black apart from a flickering light above the porch door of one of the mews houses two doors down. I tried to open it, I even shoulder barged it, but the door wouldn't move, it wouldn't budge. I shouted for help, then again and louder, but no one heard me. By then it was too late, he had closed in on me, cornering me into a cul-de-sac. He pulled the gun to eye level, his bloodshot eyes drilling into mine as blood oozed from his wound. I was staring straight down the barrel of his revolver. I pleaded with him not to shoot. Pleaded. I even offered him the money, the whole fucking ten grand, there and then, but he wouldn't listen, he just gawked at me, and then as he pulled the trigger aiming the gun to my head, I heard the sound.......

Waking up with palpitations, gasping for breath, sweat poured off me as I bolted upright from the drenched white sheet beneath me. The early morning light that seeped through the gaps in the blinds, bounced off the mirror opposite the bed and as I spotted my pale reflection, I turned to my right and noticed a note on the furrowed pillow.

Sorry baby I had to leave early as I have a morning shift. Didn't want to wake you, but I think you must have had a bad dream, cos you were sweating and talking all kinds of shit. I hope you're okay as I noticed a plaster on your stomach, I'll call you later. Love you xx

Falling back onto the dampness of the bed with my heart pounding at a pace, I spread my arms, still with the note in my right hand, closed my eyes and drew a breath or two. After a minute or so, I leant over to my left, opened the bedside table draw to see that the book and the envelope were still inside. Closing the drawer, I grabbed the company phone from under the bed and my one from the bedside table, pulled a cigarette from the packet and sparked it up. Turning both phones on, now fully charged, the business one suddenly flashed with a text message, delivered twenty minutes ago at nine thirty-seven. I took a deep breath and closed my eyes knowing it was from Mad Dog Maddox. I nervously tapped the icon with my left thumb, and the message flashed open...

I don't give a fuck how you do it, just fucking do it and finish the bastard off.

APPLE LAPTOP

HOT water from the shower poured over me as I tried to wash away the nightmare, but the dream had appeared real. I'd heard the gun shot. The fucking gunshot. I'd even felt the bullet pierce my skin. Just then, I looked down, ripped the plaster off and caressed my lower right side with the tips of my fingers. I winced as the cut from last night started to bleed again, with blood flowing down my legs, between my toes, diluting in the water, and whirling around, eventually disappearing down the plug hole.

The nightmare played over and over in my mind, as I dried myself, and placed another plaster across my wound then slipped on a pair of jeans and a black T-shirt. Paranoia started to take over with the fear of the dream becoming a reality and just then, my phone beeped again. Another message. *I've never been so popular*. Please let it be from Lisa, I thought, but out loud to myself. I hoped it would be, but no, it wasn't, it was the other one, the company phone.

Make sure you finish him off.

Stroking my four-day old stubble, I contemplated what tonight had in store as I vacated the bedroom and marched into the kitchen. Grabbing the kettle, I filled the scaly insides with the rush of cold water from the tap and tapped the knob to switch it on. Checking the phone, my one, not his, I longed for another message from Lisa, but no, just the messages about killing the bastard.

Pulling the milk from the empty fridge, it looked as lonely as my laptop that hadn't been touched at all over the past few days. Having made a mug of coffee, white, one sugar, *the usual*, I went into the lounge, sat by my wooden desk next to the bay window and stared at my closed Hewlett Packard. I really wanted an Apple laptop but could never afford one. Perhaps with the fruits of my labour, or blood money I have now, I may just treat myself. Taking a sip of coffee, my mind began shooting off in all directions about the coming night. I turned to my left and looked out of the window as the leafless trees that lined the busy street below me, swayed back and forth in the wind. Just then, I was taken elsewhere as one of my phones pinged. *Which one was it? I must sort out a different notification for each one, it would be so much easier.* It was another message. *Who was it from? Him? Lisa? Please let it be from Lisa.* I stared at both mobiles that were before me on the desk. I blew out a sigh of relieve, it was my phone, it was from Lisa. I smiled within.

Hey baby, how are you? How did you get that cut, there was blood on the sheets, and what did you dream, you were talking all kinds of crap? Are you up, are you writing? Love you xx

Lisa always encouraged me to write, and I felt guilty that I hadn't, but I felt even more remorseful about tonight. Fuck, if she only knew what I was up to. I couldn't tell her about what I was planning or my financial situation. I hadn't even known her that long, anyway I had my pride, which sounds crazy considering what I'll be doing in a few hours.

I took another sip of my coffee and pondered the questions from Lisa, whilst wishing that I'd kept a small drop of the whisky from last night to add to my coffee for a morning hit.

I went back into the kitchen to make another and as the kettle started to heat up, I messaged Lisa,

Hey baby, hope you're okay, don't worry about the cut, it's fine, I was just acting out a scene from the book I'm writing. Don't forget I'm out tonight and will probably be back late so don't wait up. Love you too xx

Then as the water came to a simmering boil, I had a moment of inspiration. I mouthed what I wrote to Lisa,

Just acting out a scene from the book I'm writing.

Taking my coffee with me I went back into the lounge, sat at my desk and with some enthusiasm, that came out of nowhere, opened my laptop. I lifted a cigarette from the packet beside my coffee, placed it between my lips, lit it, and started to tap away on the keyboard.

Chapter one

Checking the countless blurry headlights in the rear-view mirror, I caught my eye and glanced at the person staring back.

I didn't recognise myself.

Or what I imagined I was about to become.

JACK DANIELS

ONE crack on the head with a brick was all it took to bring the good looking bastard down. I felt sick with the coarse sound of his skull splitting. I'd carefully picked my moment as I hid behind a wall and waited for him to appear around the corner. He'd been out drinking most of the evening, down the pub, the Hollywood Arms, apparently his local, a two-minute walk from his house. I know that because I was there too. I'd had to size him up to see if he was bigger than me, but thankfully he was about my build and height. Nothing like Mad Dog Maddox.

I'd had two pints of Kronenbourg, which were followed by a couple of double Jack Daniels on the rocks. I'd needed some Dutch courage as I'd never killed anyone before. Saying that, I'd rarely been in a fight before. Leaving the pub with the sound of the bell ringing in last orders, just before eleven, I'd left him there propped up at the bar drinking a pint, with another waiting, bought by one of his many cronies, just with him for his money. He was pissed, talking loads of bullshit about his wealth and his women, even though he was married. This gave me a clue as to why his father-in-law, Mad Dog, wanted him dead. He sounded like such an arrogant bastard.

As soon as I left the pub, I put on a baseball cap and pushed my fingers deep into one of the pairs of surgical gloves I'd asked Lisa to get from the hospital where she worked. She'd asked why I needed them. I'd told her I was doing research for the book I was writing. She'd thought nothing further of it and had given me a pack of five. I wanted to ask if she could also bring home one of those surgeon's overalls, but I guess that would have seemed too much. So, I'd bought one of those rain macs, you know, like the ones they wear at Wimbledon when the inevitable rain stops play, or similar to the ones you see tourists wear sometimes when they've been caught out by our great British weather.

I marched from the pub, putting the white rain mac on, *boy, I looked a twat,* to a road that was around the corner from his house on Cathcart Road, which he shared with his wife, Jennifer. Apparently, as Jake had told me, the house had been bought for them by her very rich daddy, Mad Dog. I didn't have a clue how I was going pull this off, but I spotted a skip on the driveway of a house which was being refurbished, and inside the skip were bricks piled high. I looked around to make sure I wasn't being watched, thankfully the street was deserted, so I casually grabbed one, and walked the remaining distance with a brick in one hand and a knife **within** its sheath in the other.

Holding on to the brick whilst tucking the knife safely away in my inside jacket pocket, alongside some duct tape, I crouched down in a front garden, ignoring the painful fact that my right knee just clicked, behind the four-foot high garden wall of a four-storey house, out of sight, as I waited for my prey. I'd turned both mobiles to silent, as I didn't want to disturb the neighbourhood, potentially alert my victim to my presence, and just in case Mad Dog called to see if I had done the deadly deed, or Lisa wondering where the hell I was. I couldn't really tell her I was about to murder someone. *I'd think that would definitely come between us.*

It was close to half eleven. *Fuck, where's the bastard?* I bet he's had another pint or two the poor sod. I couldn't really blame him though, they were his last, although he doesn't know that.

With the house behind me dark and lifeless, it still appeared that the street sensed something evil was about to happen. Adrenaline flowed through my body from head to toe, enhancing my veins like a heavyweight boxer clenching his muscles, punching his gloves together in a ring just before going into battle with his opponent. *Have I told you I hate violence?* I can't remember the last time I had a fight. Years ago, twenty at least, and that was at school, and I lost with a whimper. So, you might ask, was I cut out for this? Was I strong enough to do this? Physically or mentally? No, of course not, but I needed the money and I'd given my word, and as I've said, you wouldn't want to go back on your word to him. Not to Mad Dog Maddox.

You might be thinking why I didn't get a job, like a normal person. Well, number one, am I normal? Number two, tell me a writer who is, and number three, you know how much he's paying me? Thousands, with many more thousands to follow at the wake.

As I've said, the cash seduced me. I'm a sucker for seduction. I'm a sucker for cash.

I looked at my phone to check the time. *Where's the bastard?* I don't wear a watch. Never have. Maybe I'll buy one with the blood money. Nothing flash like a Rolex, something simple. Those twenty minutes waiting for him took an age, especially crouching with my dodgy knee, but just then I heard footsteps in the distance. I listened hard, yes, footsteps coming my way. *It better be him. It fucking better be him. I want to get this over and done with as quick as possible.* I peered over the wall and squinted through the darkness, which was slightly distorted due to the slight drizzle and the ambient yellow glow of the light from the lamppost. Then at that moment, I spotted him and just as I thought, he was drunk. Very drunk.

Probably for the best.

This is going to be easy I thought to myself. This is going to be so fucking easy.

He was weaving side to side and staggering alone and along the pavement, arms stretched out as if for balance, mumbling to himself, walking towards me, and I suddenly felt sorry for the poor bastard, knowing that he'd just drunk his very last drink.

Unless he had a gun and used it on me, like he had in the dream last night.

With the brick in one hand **and the knife, that I'd picked** up from a hardware store earlier in the day, inside my jacket pocket, waiting to be used for the very first time, my heart belted out what felt like a drum roll as he staggered closer. I tucked myself close to the wall and there he stood, a mere foot away. Silently deep breathing to try and settle myself, which was impossible as I could hear my heart pounding within, I sensed his shadow and smelt the booze wafting past me as he ambled along on the other side of the wall, holding onto to the black wrought iron rail, trying to steady himself.

If he only knew and could see what was on the other side.

Witnessing him walk by, I ascended with an attack of guilt from behind the wall, looked around to make sure the street was quiet and silently tiptoed behind him with my heart pulverating to a level that I've never encountered before. Breathing violently but quietly, I screwed up my face aggressively, clenched the brick in my right hand, observed myself as I pulled my arm back and just like throwing a cricket ball overhand, whacked him for six, hard on the crown of his head.

The coming together of concrete cracking his skull, is a sound I will never ever forget.

He let out a yelp. Another sound that I will never forget, as he tumbled to the ground, hitting the moist pavement hard with the side of his face crashing onto the damp grey slabs. I swiftly hid back behind the wall and looked to my left and then my right. Nothing. No one. Not a murmur. The only sound I heard was my heart pounding from beneath my rib cage. With the brick still grasped in my hand, I spotted fresh blood on the corner with a piece of skin and a few brown hairs attached. I nearly vomited at the sight, as I slowly re-emerged from behind the wall, sidestepping the flower bed and cautiously approached my victim. I patted my jacket making sure my knife was still in place, knowing that any minute, I'd be finishing him off for good.

DUCT TAPE

I knelt beside him, placing the brick to my side and waiting, momentarily not believing what I'd just done. The still of the night silent, unlike my rapidly beating heart. Not a peak from any of the neighbouring houses. I looked at him and shook my head in condemnation of my own actions and mouthed, *I'm sorry.* Droplets of blood seeped from his ear creating a mazy run on the wet grey pavement, towards the drain at the side of the road. I turned him over onto his back and blood trailed across his face. He let out a moan and then another.

I don't give a fuck how you do it, just fucking do it and finish the bastard off.

With Mad Dog's blunt words of last night still sharp in my mind, I pulled the knife from my jacket and removed it from its sheath. Retrieving the duct tape from my inside jacket pocket, I sliced a strip and even though he tried to resist, bashing his head on the pavement as he did so, I covered his mouth. His eyes started to flicker, and then gradually fully opened. He looked lost and scared. His wounded head now still but to one side, covered in blood. He let out another moan. I doubled the tape across his mouth to drown out the sound, and he looked straight at me. His terrified eyes pleading with me, speaking to me to stop, but as his pupils dilated, he knew that this was his final breath.

Turning his pleading face to one side, covering his eyes, as I didn't want his tortured stare, torturing me, I clenched the knife handle for my life and plunged it, into his chest, to end his. I kept saying, *I'm sorry, I'm sorry* to myself, but it wasn't for me, it was for him. The sound of the blade slicing his skin and cracking a rib, again nearly made me vomit, as a fountain of blood appeared and sprayed in all directions.

I'm not cut out for this. I'm really not.

Thankfully the plastic mac did its job and protected my clothing from the blood spatter. I looked at him. His eyes widened, as the sound of a whimper came from beneath the brown tape that was glued to his mouth. I felt sorry for him, but he must have done something so wrong for someone to pay to have him murdered. And not just anyone, his father-in-law. Mad Dog Maddox. I didn't ask, and I didn't want to know. You just don't ask those sort of questions.

As Jake had said, "Just do the job and collect the money. Simple.*"*

Yeah! Simple.

As I hauled the knife from his dying body, blood seeped from the wound over his shirt. But there was still movement with the slight reflex of his legs and arms, and I knew I had to finish it, or I'd be finished. So, I held the knife above me, kneeling beside him, clenching the handle with both hands and plummeted the silver blade into his body so hard that the length disappeared into his ribcage.

Now, he didn't move. The job was complete. I had finished the bastard off.

Like I was asked.

Like I was told.

Like I was paid to do.

THE FINGER

WITH my blood-stained medical gloves wrapped around the seven-inch knife, I yanked it from his lifeless body, but it took two attempts for its release as it was rooted deep within his ribs and as I pulled, I heard another crack of bone. Once removed, wiping the blade on both sides across his already blood-stained shirt, I sheathed the knife and pocketed it once again, then patted his jacket and felt for his phone. Then I remembered, Mad Dog Maddox. The sick bastard wanted a photo of his dead, but still good looking son-in-law for confirmation that I've completed the job I was paid so handsomely to do. *As he keeps reminding me.* I removed the duct tape from his mouth, not wanting to leave behind anything which might somehow incriminate me, then taking out the company phone, I went to the camera icon, directed it towards the lifeless blood stained body and clicked. I looked at the image and flinched. *Did I really do that?* I looked for his contact, attached the image and pressed send.

Before I even managed to put the phone away, I received a message.

Lovely. I could actually hear Mad Dog's menacing voice saying that word.

Putting my company phone in the back pocket of my jeans, I started to search again for my victim's mobile. *There it is*. I tucked my hand inside his jacket and pulled out a gold cased, iPhone X. *It just had to be didn't it*. It was still on, still live, with seventy-five percent juice left. If it rang, I'd be up shit creak without a paddle.

I turned the phone off and placed it in one of few empty pockets remaining in my jacket. I looked up and down the silent street, slightly disturbed by the sound of a dog barking in the distance, as the glare from the streetlights accentuated the fresh red blood on the grey pavement. I dragged his lifeless body, noticing his white Nike trainers were slightly spattered with blood, over the street kerb and in between two cars, then positioned him on his side. Hidden. I stood, continually looking down at the corpse, thinking, did I really do that? Should I be proud. Am I that fucking crazy? I guess I am. But I wasn't proud. Far from it. In fact, I was feeling extremely remorseful.

Retrieving the brick from the ground, I sidestepped over the freshly drawn blood that was escaping from his body and walked away. I'd been careful not to step in the blood, not wanting to leave any incriminating footprints. That would have been a schoolboy error, something a novice would do, but I was a novice. *Oh God, please don't let me have made any stupid mistakes that could lead the police to my door.* I sauntered towards another house on the right-hand side of the road, and as I did, I hid the brick amongst many others in another skip which contained all sorts of junk from another house being refurbished. There were so many houses along this street having hundreds of thousands of pounds spent on them. *What am I thinking? Why am I thinking about property?*

Removing the bloodied rain mac, turning it inside out as I did so and carefully folding it in on itself, I stuffed it in the plastic bag that I'd brought with me for exactly this purpose, and placed it inside my jacket pocket. I crouched down behind a garden hedge and clocked the number forty which was attached to the left-hand side of the front door in cast iron figures. It was an elegant and handsome four-storey property, with a yellow exterior, blue front door and white louvered shutters either side of all the Georgian style windows. *There I go again. Describing the property. I know I used to be an estate agent, but this is crazy. Maybe I was.* I needed a cigarette. Was there time? There's always time for a smoke. I jerked the packet and with one standing out from the dwindling crowd, I clenched it between my teeth and covering the flame with my left palm, lit it, inhaling very forcefully on each take. Apparently having a smoke after you've murdered someone is like having one after a meal, well that's what Jake told me. But how would I know, as this was my first.

Once finished, diffusing the cigarette between my thumb and index finger, I placed the stub in one of my pockets and looked around onto the deserted street. I had to tell Jennifer about the murder and where he was as instructed by Mad

Dog. I pulled my phone out. What do I say? I'm sorry but I've just killed your husband. Or, I was hired by your loving father to kill your husband? I was about to message her. Then stopped. *You fucking idiot, I said quietly to myself. You stupid, stupid idiot. Not this phone. His. Use his phone.* The message wouldn't be from me, it would be from him. Well, it's his phone for a start. Yes, I said to myself, clenching my fist, it would be from him.

Closing my eyes with a shake of my head in total disbelief at what I had almost done and with a slight snigger at my stupidity I may add, I put my phone away and held his in my right hand. I stared at the black screen. *Fuck, I just turned his phone off.* I punched the right side of my head in frustration. How the hell do I turn it on. The password. Fuck. The password. I looked around. Still no one in sight. Password. *What's the password? What's the fucking password? How would I know. It's not my phone.* I thought for a minute. Then bingo. Another lightbulb moment. Yes. Got it. I looked around, still no one in sight. I quickly and quietly ran over to the body, pulled out my knife, bent down, held his right thumb and like a seasoned pro, sliced through the skin and bone, and with a snatch, detached his finger, leaving the remaining four as I placed his arm by his side. Wrapping the bloody finger in one of the gloves, I placed it inside my jacket pocket, along with the knife safely within its sheath, then ran back behind the garden wall, making sure I didn't step in any of his blood.

A fucking finger. What am I doing? But it's the only way I can get into his phone.

Hiding behind the garden wall, I felt a click in my right knee again. The same dodgy knee that has always given me jip ever since I was kicked playing football for a Sunday team, as a goalkeeper twenty years or so ago, that left me with a fractured kneecap and in plaster and hobbling on crutches for six months. I can still remember the name of the guy who dealt the blow on the pitch. It's been weak ever since, never has been the same.

The interior of the house behind me was still in darkness apart from the landing light which glared through the window giving me some much-needed light as I began to message her on his phone and not mine, shaking my head as I did so for nearly making a really stupid and fucking crucial mistake. I paused for a moment. *Shit.* I've forgotten the name of the street. What's the name of this road? I tried to remember, but the only thing I could remember was that it was a name of a Hollywood actress. Cute one at that, but who was now sadly dead. Like the fucker across the road. Fuck, what was her name? I know she was in a series, what was it, yes, Charlie's Angels, but for the life of me I couldn't remember her name. I couldn't think, I guess I had a lot on my mind. Like a murder.

I looked around the front of the house to see if there was any post laying around, even junk mail that had gone astray, but nothing. Nothing. I stepped out from the shadow of the house and went to the nearest parked car, a Range Rover, which thankfully was only a few feet away. The glow from the lamppost above gave me enough light to see if the name of the road was on the parking permit that was displayed on the inside of the windscreen. But nothing, no street name, just the council borough, Chelsea and Kensington and a few digits. What do I do? Yes, the road sign. I looked around and quickly and quietly tiptoed to the end of the road, that was only about twenty feet away. I clocked the name of the road on the street sign, Fawcett Street. *Of course, Farrah Fawcett Majors* I mumbled to myself as I ran like the Six Million Dollar Man back behind the wall. The road was still and quiet, not one person about, apart the body that was lying, on the road concealed between two cars. Two four by fours. One being a Porsche and the other a Lexus.

You could smell the money up and down this road. It just oozed wealth.

I pulled his finger out of the glove and held it between my thumb and index finger. *Which to me, looked fucking insane.* Clicking the side button to turn the phone on, I covered my jacket around it, so it wouldn't illuminate the immediate area. I tapped his finger on the home button and the phone came to life.

Once I'd placed the finger back into the glove, and back in my pocket, I scrolled through the list of contacts, I went through, A.B. Maybe he called her baby? But no. Then onto C.D.E.F.G.H, then I came to J. Jacob. Jack. James. Jamie. Jane. Jamie. Jasmine. Jason. Jemma. *There were a lot of women. I bet they're the ones he was boasting about down the pub earlier.* Scrolling further, I finally came to Jennifer. Yes, *Jennifer.* I read a few previous messages between them to make sure it was his wife, and it was. One hundred percent.

I scrolled to the final message that he'd received from her.

Please don't get too drunk like last night, if you do, you can sleep in the bloody spare room again.

He makes a habit of this.

That was sent two hours ago.

I had to think. What do I say? Tapping the phone with each thought, firstly he's been stabbed, he can't move, he's pissed, again, he's dying and he's just about to draw his last ever breath.

So, the message must only be a few words, to the point, but, as demanded by Mad Dog, I must tell her where exactly he is. At this moment I'm talking to myself again, as you can probably tell.

Okay, let's do this.

I began to type his final message.

FIVE WEEKS

SHE laid in bed, slowly drifting off to sleep, her beautiful, peaceful face slightly tilted to the left, with her blond hair spread like a peacock's tail on the freshly laundered, plump, white goose down pillows. The latest book that had her turning the pages quicker than she was reading them, was loosely held in her hand, resting on her perfect breasts, moving to the rhythm of her silent breathing, when suddenly her peace was shattered by the sound of her mobile phone vibrating on the bedside table.

Startled she sat upright as the glare from the screen illuminated the semi-darkness. The paperback, Five Weeks, fell onto the white, wooden floor and as it did, closed itself. She picked up her phone and twelve zero five a.m. flashed before her, along with a text and the name of her husband. The white background highlighting the bold black font.

Her mouth opened simultaneously along with her widening, sleepy eyes as she stared at the message.

She rubbed her ocean blue eyes in disbelief and re-read the message.

Help, I've been stabbed on Fawcett Street.

She paused. Not quite believing what she was reading. Shock **registered on** her face, then her expression drew to panic.

Within seconds she jumped out of bed, threw on the tracksuit that was draped over the back of the wicker chair in the corner of the bedroom, slipped her well-manicured feet into a pair of trainers, grabbed her mobile, sprinted downstairs and jumped the last four steps, twisting her ankle as she landed.

She winced at the pain.

Without closing the door behind her, she ran with a limp in the light drizzle, the short distance, to find him.

As she turned into Fawcett Street, I spotted her for the very first time as I squatted behind a wall. She did look like a Jennifer. Tall. Slim. Blond. Beautiful. In a grey tracksuit, looking petrified. Three minutes, give or take a few seconds from when she'd received the message, from his phone which now was switched off.

It was now early Monday morning, wet, cold and grey just like the pavement she stood on. She was alone on the street, apart from me, hiding behind the wall of one of the four-story Georgian style townhouses that lined this affluent residential road.

Her pace faltered from the pain of her twisted ankle, as she ran frantically up the middle of the road looking from left to right to try and find her husband, until she spotted the body hidden in-between the black Porsche and silver Lexus. Was it him? She didn't want to believe it. It could have been a mistake. She had only received a text message, and that could have come from anyone. And it had. Me. And even with the yellow glow from the streetlights above highlighting the body, she still couldn't be sure.

But I knew. I knew it was him. The poor bastard.

She looked around for any sign of life. Nothing. Silence. Apart from the continuous glare from the streetlamps breaking the darkness.

The bite in the wind sent another shiver down my spine as she got closer to the body. Tears continued to fill her frightened eyes, escaping down her perfect cheekbones. Her hand covered her mouth and she let out a blood curdling scream as she finally recognised him, even though he was lying on his side with his face turned away. That was the way I'd positioned him. I hadn't wanted her to see his dead eyes, as she approached him.

Her own eyes were soaked with tears, her blond hair and face moist from the light rain. As she drew closer to the still body, concealed between two cars, she came to a complete halt as she gasped for air. The guilt inside me was overwhelming as I observed the horror on her innocent face.

She paused as she stood over him. It was him. I knew that, but now she knew.

She froze for a second, trying to **take it all in**.

Shaking with fear she crouched down and knelt beside him. Her tears falling, amalgamating with the blood that had escaped from his body which now surrounded her as it absorbed into her grey tracksuit bottoms.

She lifted his head and cradled it in her arms, pushing his fringe to one side and staring into his lifeless eyes.

"My God. No. No," she screamed, sobbing hysterically. "Help me. Somebody please help me."

As she yelled for help, houses on either side of the tree-lined street began to light up, with rooms on all floors illuminating the previously dark and peaceful road. Front doors, first, second and third floor sash windows began to open with people looking to see what the commotion was.

"Someone help me. He's dead. He's been stabbed. Please someone help me," she cried, looking around for anyone as her blond hair, now stained in places with blood, swept across her face.

I wanted to go over and comfort her, to put my arm around her, even hug her, to tell her everything would be okay, but of course I knew that would be sick.

Anyway, I didn't want to be the first on the scene, even though I was.

Just then, looking at her, I felt a huge pang of guilt, I really did, but as Jake, and Mad Dog Maddox had said, he'd deserved it. I don't know what he'd done, apart from the affairs he'd boasted about in the pub, or why he'd had to be killed, but one day I hoped to find out and I hoped she would understand why he had to be murdered. Why I murdered him.

A couple in their mid-thirties, from one of the houses, came out to investigate. Then another and another. They all seemed to be the same age. How on earth do they afford these houses? The shock on their faces at what they were seeing before them was probably the same shocked look they would have when they received their monthly mortgage statements. We were in an ultra-wealthy part of London, many of these multi-million-pound houses would have already unearthed the basements to create swimming pools or cinema rooms. *I can't believe I'm thinking about property again.* I assumed that the homeowners in this fashionable and well-heeled part of London hadn't seen a dead body outside their houses before. If there ever had been, it hadn't been in their lifetime.

She was now surrounded by good Samaritans. I liked that. A lady in a dressing gown put a blue patterned blanket around her shoulders as the first sound of police sirens escalated in the distance. I swept out of the shadow of the wall onto the street to mingle and try not to look out of place. There was now a crowd of around twenty people surrounding her, with the dead body still in full view and thankfully, many various size bloody footprints now embellishing the scene. I spotted a sick bastard taking a photo of my handy work on his mobile. I wondered if he'd post the image up on social media, maybe Twitter, with its own hashtag. A police car with its flashing blue lights came to a halt. And then another, with an ambulance tailing behind. *It was a bit late for an ambulance.*

The police, there were six in total, cordoned off the crime scene with the usual yellow and black, 'DO NOT CROSS THE LINE' tape. And I'm sure there will be a tent covering the dead body and immediate area shortly. Like they do on TV cop shows, like Luther. The concerned and shocked residents were asked to return to their plush houses. Two or three lingered, but the crowds were disbursing gradually. A policewoman comforting Jennifer led her into the rear of one of the police cars. Another huge slice of guilt hit me just then. She was hysterical as she bent down and disappeared into the darkness of the car.

At that moment, I knew that I had to disappear too.

GOODFELLAS

TURNING right out of Fawcett Street and along Redcliffe Gardens towards Old Brompton Road, I heard sirens in the background and even a chopper above in the damp early morning sky. This made my heart beat even faster as I knew that they would be looking for the killer. Me. With the helicopter circulating over the streets of West London, it reminded me of one of my favourite films, *Goodfellas.* You know, the scene where Ray Liotta was out driving around the city, distributing coke, whilst his brother in the wheelchair was at home stirring the spaghetti sauce.

I checked my phone and noticed a text from Lisa saying goodnight. Keeping my baseball cap slanted forward covering my face and my collar up, I headed down to the nearest underground station, which was Earls Court. But it was closed. The last train was at eleven forty five. Passing the station, I walked further up Earls Court Road until I hit Cromwell Road, and as I did, I checked Google to see how long it would take to walk back to West Hampstead. At least I had a signal and fifty percent left on my phone this time. The walk back to my flat in West Hampstead was about an hour and thirty minutes and it was now a few minutes to one. A few minutes has been all it had taken to end a life of around thirty years. At that moment I received a text message on the company phone, which brought me to a halt.

Nice job.

Mad Dog.

Reading his message, a pain stabbed me in the heart. I placed my hand against it and squeezed my chest. I suddenly was consumed by guilt as my mind began to strike off in all directions. *Fuck, what have I done?* I felt a twinge lower down. I lifted my top and the plaster that had been holding my cut together had vanished. I ran my palm over the wound, disturbing some dried blood and causing the cut to weep again, as I walked along a London street, ironically like a policeman on the beat. A few streets back there were plenty about at that moment. I became paranoid hoping that I hadn't left a trace at the scene. But I couldn't go back, no way, not with the police everywhere.

Anyway, it would be murder there now.

The police helicopter was still circling in the distance as I walked, with speed onto Ladbroke Grove. Even at this hour there were people milling around, chatting on the streets, drinking and smoking spliffs. I inhaled the early morning air as the smell of marijuana circulated around me. I loved that smell and I was tempted to buy an eighth of weed. I hadn't smoked weed for years. *What a time to start again.* As I walked past a cab rank, I noticed two black dudes behind the glass-fronted counter rolling a joint each. I really could do with a smoke. I really could, and you know what? After the night I'd had, I thought what the fuck, I might as well. I calmly stepped inside the building and more or less, within three minutes walked out with a bag of weed and a couple of ready rolled joints.

As I lit one and took the first drag, the sensation hit me immediately. I marched towards Kilburn High Street. Kill being an appropriate word. I could still hear the sound of his cracking skull as I whacked the brick over his head.

I took another hit of the weed to try and dull the memory.

Fifteen minutes and a second joint later, I was fast pacing it down West End Lane to the mansion of flats that awaited me. The chill dampness of the early November morning cut through me like the knife cutting through the man I'd just stabbed. As I opened and closed the main front door to the building behind me, I felt safe for the first time since I'd left the crime scene. I checked my phone. No further messages from him. It was just before three. I crept up the communal stairs with the hideous coloured carpet playing games with my stoned mind and bloodshot eyes, and slowly, and quietly opened the flat door. Popping my head around the bedroom door to check that Lisa was asleep, which she was, I tiptoed across the tiny hallway into the kitchen and closed the door.

I stood with my back and head tilted against the door, eyes closed and drew a deep breath, with my arms falling either side of me. As I stood in silence, my mind manually replayed the night's events and almost automatically, the hairs on the back of my neck rose. Stiffness suddenly gripped my shoulders and I manoeuvred them round and round, like coupling rods on a train, to release the strain, but then the notion of what I had done stopped me in my tracks.

CATERPILLAR

THE room was spinning before me as I opened my eyes. I felt dizzy. Sick. I wanted a whisky, but I'd finished that last night. I went over to the fridge hoping to find something alcoholic inside. I opened it. Yes. I quietly said out loud, clenching my fist. Lisa had bought a six pack. What a good girl, I don't deserve her. I ripped open a can and sat down as I took a couple of well-deserved gulps of the amber nectar. You know, like coming home after a hard day at the office. But this time I hadn't been negotiating a property deal. I'd exchanged and completed on a murder.

"Murder," I whispered. "A fucking murder."

Emptying my many pockets, I laid out on the table before me, three mobile phones. *Two days ago, I'd had one, now I had three.* The knife, the duct tape and the bag with its gruesome contents, including the finger.

I noticed a message on the company phone. It was silent but vibrating.

Fuck it. It can wait.

Pulling out the bag of weed, and papers along with my cigarettes, I prepared to roll another joint. I pulled a king-size rizla out of the green packet and laid it on the table. Licking the seam of the cigarette, I opened it and poured the tobacco along the crease of the paper. Opening the bag of weed, I crumbled an amount over the tobacco, mixed it up, picked up the paper and rolled it between my two thumbs and index fingers. Having licked the papers closed, I ripped some of the rizla package to make a roach, sat back and sparked the joint up. That first intake of smoke swirled around my brain and then I took another drag.

The phone vibrated again. Another message. *Bollocks.* Picking the phone up, I pressed the icon.

Where are you?

I took another drag of the joint. Do I answer? Of course, I do. I have too.

At home. I replied.

Good. Stay there. Do not leave. My sources tell me the fucking pigs are everywhere.

I replied.

I wasn't intending to.

Continuing to smoke the joint, I chased it down with another beer. I looked at the clock, it was now approaching four in the morning. In a couple of hours Lisa would be moaning at the sound of the alarm on her mobile phone before reaching out from beneath the duvet to turn it off. Finishing the joint then dropping it into the beer can, I thought about how I was going to dispose of the bag, as I stared at it along with the phones, knife and duct tape, and just then I had a sudden grotesque notion to look at the accessories to my crime. I opened last night's Evening Standard that Lisa had brought home, laid it out on the table and poured the grisly bag contents onto it. Gloves. Mac, and the finger which I pulled from one of the gloves. A Finger. *A fucking finger.* I was now so stoned, I began to hallucinate and I swear, for a split second I spotted the finger crawl across the table like a caterpillar. I wrapped the finger in one of the unused gloves that Lisa had given me, but I still had to get rid of the blood stained mac, gloves and tape. Come on man, think. Think. Then, just then, I had one of those lightbulb moments. Got it. I'll drive Lisa to work, to the hospital and get rid of the items there. I'll put the bag of contents in one of the bins. Surgical gloves, bloody mac, even the tape, they wouldn't be any of the wiser. Brilliant. But the knife. What about the knife? I walked over to the sink, **removed the knife from its sheath, which I placed in the bag to get rid of,** ran the hot water over it, covered it with a generous amount of Fairy Liquid and scrubbed away any blood that remained. I then wiped the knife dry and placed in the cutlery drawer. Lisa wouldn't know the difference. I'm sure she wouldn't.

Putting the mac, gloves and duct tape back into the bag, I stuffed it into my jacket. Time was ticking, it was now four fifteen and if I was going to drive Lisa to work and get rid of the evidence, I really should try to get some shut-eye or try and relax. Relax? Even having smoked weed there was no chance. I'd just committed a crime. A murder. Having cleared the table, I went for a piss, got undressed and without making a sound, got into bed with Lisa asleep beside me. I turned all phones off, put the company and the gold cased one in the drawer, and placed the glove with the finger in too, next to the remaining three gloves.

Checking that the envelope of cash was still hidden beneath the book, I laid on my back, head spinning, staring into darkness, with a slight glow from the streetlight coming through the crack in the blinds and with Lisa's gentle deep breathing to comfort me.

THE KNIFE

"BABY, baby."

I jerked as I felt Lisa's warm palm on my sweaty, thumping chest.

"Baby, you had another bad dream."

"Did I?" I replied with my eyes still closed.

"Yes, you were mumbling all sorts of shit again. Are you okay?"

"Yeah, I guess, just lots on my mind, you know the book and everything."

"That editor of yours. She'll be the death of you."

"She's doing me a big favour but she has a very tight schedule."

"I know, I know. Look I'd better have a shower. Have to leave shortly. Oh, how's the cut by the way?"

"Oh, its fine, nothing to worry about. I thought I'd drive you to work this morning."

"Really? You look like you could do with some more sleep?"

"Yes really, I'm fine."

"That would be nice. You can tell me all about last night."

"Yes of course."

I may miss out a few details.

She turned towards me, her brown flowing hair brushing my face as she gave me a kiss and then with a spin she rolled out of bed and I watched her slim naked body appear from under the duvet and out the door towards the bathroom. I laid back down for a moment. Stretched my arms as I yawned and breathed heavily. The adrenalin hadn't settled, the rush was real. *What have a done?* I whispered to myself, as I pushed my hair back across my scalp.

"Hey baby, shall I keep the shower running for you?"

Lisa shouted from the bathroom.

"Yeah, sure, thanks, coming now."

Shit, the weed!

I threw the duvet off, slipped out of bed, turned on my phone and checked the drawer contents. I pondered turning the company phone on but decided against it until I was alone. I made my way to the kitchen to pick up the weed from last night off the table, placed it in my desk drawer in the lounge, then proceeded into the bathroom bypassing Lisa on the way.

She knew I'd smoked the green stuff years ago, but thought I'd given it up!

Well, I had until last night.

She would not approve.

"I'm sticking the kettle on, want a cuppa?"

"Is the pope Catholic? I'll be five minutes."

Closing my eyes, I felt the flow of the hot water try and seek out and cleanse my guilt. But that was impossible. The guilt was rooted within.

"Babe, coffee's ready," Lisa shouted from the other side of the door.

"Okay, just finishing up."

I turned off the shower, but I could have stayed beneath forever, feeling safe, behind the frosted shower screen with the calming flow of water beating down on me.

Once dried and dressed I went into the kitchen. Victims by Culture Club was playing on the radio. *Just had to be.* Lisa and I were suckers for 80's music. Lisa, with a mug of coffee in one hand and a slice of toast in the other, was dressed in her nurses uniform. She looked very sexy. Sometimes, when I was feeling perverted, I'd ask her to role play, you know, me being the patient and she the nurse, but that was for another time. I looked at the plate on the table. Two further slices, buttered.

Sandwiches, that she makes every morning for her lunch, also on the table wrapped in foil.

"I couldn't find a clean knife, so I had to use that new one to slice the tomatoes for my sandwiches. When did you get it?" she said as she pointed to the drainer.

Fuck. She used the knife. *Jesus.*

"I bought it the other day. Thought we could do with another one."

"Another one to the collection, it's nice and sharp. Have some toast baby."

"No, it's okay, I'm not really hungry at the moment, I'll have something when I get back."

"Okay baby, we'd better get going, you know how the traffic can be, even this early."

Just then, the beeps on the hour, on the radio, announced the morning news.

"Police have confirmed that the body of a man in his mid to late thirties has been found in a West London street. It is thought he died from a knife attack late last night."

My heart sank. *Shit. Fuck. Fuck. Fuck.*

"Oh my God, how dreadful. Poor man. That's another stabbing and pointless death in London," Lisa said as she packed her sandwiches in her rucksack.

"Sorry?"

"The news, just now," she reiterated, "that someone has been stabbed to death in West London."

"Oh right, yes. Sorry, I was miles away."

"You okay baby, you, you seem, I don't know, not with it."

"Yes, I'm fine, just thinking about what I have to do today."

"Writing a bestseller, I hope."

"Yes baby, a bestseller. God, you can read me like a book."

"Very droll."

"Come on, let's take you to work."

Making sure the bag of evidence was still in my jacket, I quickly ran into the bedroom, opened the drawer, picked up a clean pair of surgical gloves and grabbed the company phone. I turned it on, switched it to silent and placed it in my inside my jacket pocket.

"Come on babe, I'll be late, you know what the traffic can be like."

"I'm coming, just need a quick pee."

"Okay you have one minute. I'm counting."

"Not too fast."

Closing the bathroom door behind me, I lifted up the toilet seat. Kneeling before it, I vomited, flushing at the same time to drown out the noise. The thought of driving Lisa to work as an excuse to get rid of the evidence from last night's murder momentarily hit me.

"Baby, we have to go, now." I heard her shout.

Staring into the bathroom mirror at the reflection of a murderer, I turned on the tap, cupped some water within my hands, splashed my face and washed my mouth out. At that moment I was taken back a quarter of a century to when my mum washed my mouth out with soap and water for telling a ten year old girl, who lived down the road, to fuck off.

"Baby, come on, we've got to go."

"Sorry baby, coming," I shouted, as I grabbed my baseball cap, leaving the radio on in the kitchen, playing Guilty by Barbra Streisand and Barry Gibb.

EVENING STANDARD

"THIS is nice baby, we should do it more often, you know, driving me to work, at least the traffic isn't as bad as I thought it would be."

"Yes, maybe we should, at least it gets me out of bed at a reasonable hour, to write more, which I have to do with that deadline looming."

"Yep, that bestseller baby. No pressure," she laughed as I felt a vibration beating terror against my heart. *The company phone, it's him.*

"I'm joking baby."

"I know you are, but I want to, no I need to get it finished."

"Well that's down to you. The more you write every day, the quicker you'll be signing books at Waterstones."

I felt another vibration against my chest. *Fuck what does he want? I can't deal with this.* I can't check now, Lisa will see and ask why I have another phone.

"So handy that you live only a fifteen minute drive away from the hospital. I could get really used to you being my chauffeur if I moved in."

"I bet you could, just call me James."

Lisa laughed and rested her hand on my leg.

"But you don't live too far from work. Anyway, you wouldn't want to live in my flat, it's a dump, as you know. Let's get the book published first and then see."

"Is that a polite way of saying you don't want to live with me full time?"

"Don't be silly babe, it's just that…"

I've murdered someone, and I don't want you involved.

"What baby?"

"Well, it's a dump and far too small and far too bloody expensive."

"Yeah, I know, I just wanted to see your reaction."

"Oh, testing me now, are we?"

Like I need testing at this moment.

"No baby don't be silly," Lisa replied, as we approached the hospital.

"Here we are."

"Thanks baby. I'd better shoot, shift starts in five minutes, have a good day of writing. Oh, before I forget, I have to stay home tonight, the girls are planning a surprise birthday party for a colleague at work, they want to have a chat about it."

"With a bottle or two, I'm sure."

"You know them. I'll call you later."

"Okay, have a good day."

We kissed goodbye and I watched her disappear behind the automatic double doors at the entrance of the hospital. As soon as Lisa was out of sight, I immediately pulled the company phone from my inside jacket pocket and pressed the home button. The phone came to life. Two messages. My heart stopped.

First message: *Your murder is all over the news.*

Don't I know it.

My heart sank reading that word. MURDER.

Second message: *Where are you?*

Who the fucking hell does he think he is, my mother? My poor mum. She had died, along with my dad, in a tragic car accident, which wasn't their fault, it was a drunk driver. A kid, early teens, pissed and stoned out of his head. I'd been in my early twenties at the time. I was an only child. No siblings and my grandparents were dead too. No other family, which at this moment, suited me right down to the ground.

What should I say? I'm getting rid of the evidence and where?

No. No. I can't. He'll question it.

I've just driven my girlfriend to work and now I'm heading back home.

Message sent.

I drove around the hospital, passing rows of cars parked in the overpriced car park. I shook my head. *People have to pay to see their sick and dying relatives and friends.* I felt the vibration of the phone again. Ignoring it, I spotted a row of eight yellow commercial bins, all with clinical waste written on them, next to each other in a brick covered area. I drove back to the main entrance and parked outside. I had five free minutes to get rid of the evidence. I didn't have the three quid on me to pay for the parking. I chortled within. I had ten grand in cash back home, but no loose change on me. I looked around. There were people mingling outside, smoking. Jesus, patients with drips or in wheelchairs smoking outside the hospital.

If you're going to get cancer, I guess this is the most convenient place to get it.

But it causes such a strain on NHS resources and finances. Then again, who am I to talk, puffing away like a chimney.

I could do with one now but having been in a rush to leave this morning I'd left them behind. I even checked the glove compartment, but not a single cigarette was hiding inside, just empty packets that I'd gathered up from the floor, before Lisa stepped into the car earlier.

With people visiting their loved ones, wandering to and from their cars to the hospital and back again, I ducked down to try and make myself look small, as I sidled towards the bins. Putting on a pair of the surgical gloves that I'd taken from the drawer earlier, I played out a game in my head. *What a time to play games.* Which bin should I chose? *Ip, dip sky blue who's it not you. It's not the middle one. Ip, dip sky blue who's it not you.* It's the right one. I lifted the lid of the bin, which had a broken lock. As I picked up the bag I was just about to set it into the waste and tuck it out of sight, but just then had another lightbulb moment. I decided I would use three bins, yes, three separate bins, and thankfully three out of the eight bins had broken locks. So, I quickly pulled the mac out and put that amongst the crap in one of the right-hand bins. Then I pulled out the roll of tape, along with the loose pieces that I'd put across his mouth and hid them underneath all sorts of rubbish in a middle bin. Then I placed in one of the left-hand bins the knife sheath and the gloves that I'd worn when I killed the poor bastard who was making all the news this morning. I looked around as I closed the lid. All clear. No one in my immediate view. As I walked back towards the car, placing the empty bag in my jacket pocket, I checked the company phone to read the message from earlier.

Don't get caught.

It's not on my agenda this morning, I said out loud as I responded.

I'll try not to. I replied.

Driving back, the early morning traffic along West End Lane was now bumper to bumper, so I parked the car on a side street about a mile away from my flat. As I strolled along

West End Lane, quicker than the snail pace of the cars to my right, I pulled down my baseball cap to cover my guilt. I passed the familiar range of shops along this busy and popular high street, with its restaurants, supermarkets, independent cafés, as well as the branded coffee shops, and many of my favourite charity shops. I really wanted to call in for an espresso, a hit of much needed coffee, but I didn't have the bottle. *I didn't have the bottle. But I had the bottle for murder.* Flinging the empty bag into one of the many bins that lined the street, and passing West Hampstead underground station, I picked up a copy of Metro, the free morning paper that commuters read in their millions and discard on the train upon exiting, ready to be read by others. I scanned the front page. Nothing. I licked my fingertips at each turn of the page. Nothing. Not a word. *What, after what I've been through, my crime is not newsworthy?* Of course, it's too early. But I bet your bottom dollar, it will be front page news in the Evening Standard later.

MANHATTAN

ARRIVING back at the flat, I opened the main door and hesitantly peeked in the pigeonhole for any post, as I closed the door behind me. A collection of white but mainly brown envelopes greeted me. Fourteen letters in total. All final and threatening demands from bailiffs and loan sharks indicating that they'd be knocking on my door to remove items of furniture or breaking my legs if outstanding debts were not paid immediately.

As I climbed the stairs to my flat, I stuffed them into my jacket pocket to try and forget about them, thinking they would go way, you know, like burying your head in the sand.

That reminds me. The funeral, the wake.

I'll be receiving a text about that soon.

Pacing the living room floor with a much needed cigarette, smoke following my every move and the radio still on in the kitchen, informing me it was just after nine, my mind replayed the events of last night in all its ultra-high definition. I decided to open my laptop. If I have to write this book, I'd better get on with it. So, with a fresh steaming cup of coffee and music playing in the background to keep me company, I continued where I had left off the day before.

The words were flowing from my fingertips via the keyboard and onto the fifteen inch screen before me. The words flowed and flowed, like his blood last night. I got to the part where I'd just killed him and was about to message his wife. I didn't have to invent characters, plots or locations. This story was real.

The excitement running through my veins as I wrote every living word, caught my breath, and before I knew it, I looked at the word count. Five thousand, three hundred and twenty-four words. I lit yet another cigarette and sat back to read what I had written.

Then reality sank in as I read. This isn't fiction. This is real. There was no way I could get away with publishing this. It was a full on confession. I would get caught. I would get arrested. Would it be a first? An author who kills, then writes about it, and the book becomes a #1 international bestseller, or even a movie. What was I thinking? I needed to change names and locations. I crashed out the cigarette in the overflowing ashtray and checked my emails. One was from my editor in America that she'd sent a few hours ago. What timing.

Hey, how's it going, just thought I'd see if you have anything for me?

Before I had a chance to type a reply, the phone rang. I recognised the number. It was the estate agent. I was sure they were calling about the overdue rent. Of course, I was right.

"Hello."

"Oh, good morning, its Justin from the letting agents."

"Oh, hi there."

"Is it convenient to talk?"

"Yes."

"It's about the overdue rent." *Told you.* "It's getting rather serious I'm afraid, it's now three months, and......."

"Yes, I know, it's fine, I'll be in today with the cash," I snapped back.

"Cash? You do know how much it is, don't you?"

"Three months' worth."

"Yes, but the amount?"

"Tell me."

"Three thousand, seven hundred and fifty pounds to be precise."

To be precise! But I guess he was only doing his job. Like I'd done mine last night.

"Fine."

"Fine?"

"Yes fine. I'll be in later this afternoon, about two."

"Excellent. I look forward to seeing you then."

As I pressed the end call icon, I looked around the room.

Four fucking thousand for this shithole.

Oh, fuck, my editor.

Hey, guess what, I have a few chapters for you. I'm going to reread what I've written and make a couple of changes, then I'll email it to you later today, you should have them when you wake up.

The phone pinged. Text message. I was bought back to reality, after having escaped to my fictional (or not so fictional) world for a few minutes, it was the company phone.

Meet me here tonight at 10. Memorise location and delete.

What the fuck. Why. Jesus Christ.

I wrote the location down. It was somewhere near Heathrow. Another hour-long journey. Better not be raining. Bloody wipers.

Okay. I answered.

Tapping away on my keyboard, I came to the scene where I spotted the attractive widower. *Her eyes soaked with tears, her blond hair and face moist from the light rain. As she drew closer to the still body, laying, concealed between two cars, she came to a complete halt as she gasped for air. The guilt inside me was overwhelming as I observed her frightened and innocent face.*

Finishing that particular scene, I began to read what I had written. A story of a seriously debt-ridden author, being threatened by loan shark thugs, who somehow got mixed up with a bunch of people he would never usually associate with in a million years. Being paid handsomely to kill the son-in-law of a known East End criminal, who was also a successful businessman. You couldn't make it up. I hadn't. This was real.

As I went through the text I changed various details which could identify me as the murderer. My first idea was to relocate the entire story to New York. I looked up some areas on Google. I lived in an apartment on Upper East Side, Manhattan, with Lexington Av-63 Street subway station my nearest underground. The dilapidated building in Buckinghamshire was located in Vince Lombardi service area, about a thirty minute drive from Manhattan and across the George Washington Bridge. Lisa was called Rachel and the hospital she worked at was the Lenox Hill on 100 E 77th St.

My Golf was a Honda and like in real life, I used to work in real estate. Mad Dog was called Bulldog, Jennifer was now Monica and Hancock Street, an affluent location in Bedford Stuyvesant was the road on which the murder took place. Apparently, as confirmed by the Brooklyn Daily Eagle, homicides were up by two hundred percent last year in parts of Bedford Stuyvesant. Prefect for my murder and story. Also, The Metro paper was replaced by the A M New York, the Evening Standard was now The Manhattan Times and the pound was of course dollars.

Thank fuck for Google.

Emailing what I had written to my editor, I paced into kitchen to make another coffee. I could've done with something stronger, but I had a meeting tonight and I had to keep my wits about me. As the kettle came to a boil, so did further confirmation of what I'd done last night, as the three o'clock news came on the radio.

"Met Police have confirmed that the man, in his mid-thirties, who was found dead last night in Fawcett Street, West London, died of multiple stab wounds. Police were called to the incident just after twelve thirty this morning and are still at the scene. No arrests have been made at the present time and police are urging any witnesses to come forward."

Fuck. The first word that came out of my mouth. This is not me. I'm not a murderer. I'm an author. I'm just not up for this. I went back to my laptop and wrote about how I was feeling. How I had just listened to the news.

Then my phone rang. Shit.

The estate agent.

"Yes, hello."

"It's Justin from West End Lane Estate Agents."

I know. Trust me.

"I was just wondering if you are still coming into the office to pay the outstanding rent today as discussed?"

"Hi, yes, sorry, running late. I'll be with you by three-thirty, okay."

"Perfect see you then."

Closing the call, I pulled out another cigarette from the dwindling pack before me. I lit it and drew a deep breath and as I inhaled, I felt the smoke penetrate my lungs. I thought about rolling a joint, but I was afraid paranoia would set in and the way I was feeling at that very moment, a spliff could tip me over the edge. Sitting back into the creaky old wooden chair, I put my hands out in front of me. They trembled as the cigarette continued to burn between my index and middle fingers. As I stared at my quivering hands, I had a flashback to last night. *The crack on the head. Stabbing in the chest. Mutilation of his finger.* Killing the cigarette within the sea of dead filters in the ashtray, I held my head in the palm of my hands, as I rested my elbows on the table. A cool shiver played tag along my curved spine as I pictured the devastating scene and images of the bloody dead body came back to haunt me.

Pinching my inner eyes with my thumb and index finger, blobs of different colours played out before me. As I continued to squeeze, scintillating and rapidly moving grid-like patterns, reminiscent of psychedelic paintings, appeared. I was disturbed, as the phone sounded again, it was another message. Opening my moist guilt-ridden eyes, as the rain started to patter the sash window, I checked the message, it was from Lisa.

Hey baby, hope the writing is going well. Thank you for driving me to work this morning, we must do that more often. Love you L xx

My heart sank. I wish I could turn back the clock, but it was too late. I had committed the crime, and not just any crime. As I was about to message her back, I noticed the time on the phone. Twenty past three. *Shit, the estate agents.* I went into the bedroom, opened the draw, trying to ignore the slightly blood-stained surgical glove with the finger in it, picked up the book, pulled out the envelope beneath it and sat on the bed. Pulling out four bundles of cash, each containing a thousand pounds, I removed five fifty pound notes from one bundle and stuffed them back in the envelope, which I replaced under the book in the drawer. I grabbed my jacket, baseball cap and made my way to the estate agents up the road.

The rain continued to fall, a light drizzle, as I passed West Hampstead tube station. As I paced, I was stopped in my tracks. I spotted in big black font, on the front page of the Evening Standard,

"MAN MURDERED IN WEALTHY LONDON STREET."

My story. I'm published. Will my book be?

Grabbing a copy, I swiftly turned to page two and scanned the report. My heart beating faster with each word. Murder. Stabbing. Fatal. Dead. The last sentence, if anyone knows anything or saw anything, please contact the police.

The words in the paper blurred before me. Closing it, I shoved the paper in the first bin I came across on the street. The rain started to fall slightly heavier as I turned my collar up and tilted my cap, trying to hide myself, but that was impossible. I felt like I was a man on the run. A man wanted. And I was.

People, with umbrellas, ambling along West End Lane, were making their way to the tube station, picking up copies of the Evening Standard, completely oblivious that in a few minutes, they'd be reading about a murder committed by the guy they'd just walked past. I sparked up another cigarette. I had sick thoughts of getting on the tube, sitting next to them or opposite, observing their expressions as they read the story on the front and inside pages, totally unaware that they were reading about me. The murderer. I decided against it. I crushed the half smoked cigarette out in a puddle as I arrived at the estate agents.

Holding my breath as I opened the door, I asked for Justin. He was having a coffee and reading a newspaper. *Busy day.* No need to guess what free paper he was reading as he folded it and placed it by his phone on his desk. The headlines stared straight back at me. I handed over the exact amount in crisp fifty-pound notes. The money I'd been paid for the murder which was making all the headlines. It almost killed me to hand over nearly four thousand pounds. *Believe me.* He asked me to wait and offered me a seat for a moment as he went into the back office to count it. He felt it was too risky to count this amount of money in full view of the street, with the rise in crime. *Funny that.* He returned with a receipt and handed it over to me. We shook hands and that was that. I left the office, out onto the busy high street and made my way back to the flat that I was now up to date with the rental payments on.

At that moment I felt like a normal human, paying rent and with money to settle other bills, at least I did, until I returned to my flat, with a message waiting for me on the company phone.

VAMOS

YOU *did take his phone, didn't you, like I asked you to?*

I swear, I could hear him saying those words, like he was in the room, standing next to me, blowing cigar smoke in my face, his penetrating eyes digging into mine.

I started to shake. Sweat began to run down my forehead. Pacing each room in the flat, which didn't take long, as it was so small, the phone in my hand pinged again before I could even answer him.

Well?

Yes, like you asked, why?

I waited for his reply. I lit up another cigarette as I did so. My heart beating to every drag I sucked in.

Ping.

You ask why?

Few seconds later, it pinged again.

Never ask me why? And whatever you do, DO NOT TURN THE THING ON. OKAY?

It hasn't been on, only when I messaged your daughter.

Another ping.

Keep it that way. 10 sharp. DON'T BE LATE.

No, I won't.

The phone pinged yet again.

And bring the finger.

I stabbed out the cigarette that I'd smoked in record time right down to the filter. I went into the bedroom, opened the drawer to make sure the phone was off, and it was. I sat on the bed. Head held in the palms of my hands, I looked at Lisa's alarm clock. It was close to half four. I wondered how long it would be till the police came knocking on the door. I laid on the bed with my arms behind my head. Fucking hell, what had I done? I knew what I'd done, but why had I done it? I knew exactly why I'd done it. I can't go back now. I can't return the money and say forget it. Four grand has already vanished. *Bloody rent.* Maybe I should vanish. This minute. *Vamos.* Get a plane ticket and go, go anywhere, abroad. Leave a note for Lisa. But I'd be a fugitive on the run, and not just running away from the police, but him. And anyway, he would find me. And then, no doubt, kill me.

FRANKIE GOES TO HOLLYWOOD

HI baby, hope your day was okay. Have fun tonight. I'm going out soon to see a mate who I haven't seen for ages. I'll message you when I'm back home xx

If I make it home.

The queue at the petrol station on Finchley Road was four cars deep. On each pump. The petrol light had made an appearance as soon as I'd turned the key. I had a fair distance to drive, and the tank was running on empty, unlike my adrenaline. I detest getting fuel. It's not the money, that was currently no object, it's the inconvenience, especially as it had started to rain again as soon as I left the flat. Relax by Frankie Goes to Hollywood was playing out from the car radio. Relax! As if! Relaxing was the furthest thing from my mind, as was Hollywood. The car ahead of me drove off and I inched forward.

Filling the car with unleaded, I went to pay, passing copies of the Evening Standard displayed on the counter with the headlines following me. Having paid with cash, I bought a bottle of Jack Daniels for later, jumped back into the car and exited north back onto Finchley Road.

The rain began to hammer down as I steered from the A41 onto the North Circular. It was just after nine thirty as I drove onto the unusually quiet M4. The driving rain increased with my one wiper doing a two-man job. *Why didn't I get this fixed?* I've got the money now. *Fucking idiot.* My vision, hindered by the fall of rain hitting the windscreen, became blurred, as I drove in semi-darkness, with just the dim illumination of the motorway lights to guide me.

I felt alone on the road with not a single car ahead, or to my side. I liked that. I purposely turned down the news on the radio when it came on as I didn't want to be reminded of my crime. Junction four was a quarter of a mile away and I was about to indicate when suddenly, out of nowhere, blue flashing lights appeared in my rear-view mirror. *Oh fuck. Is that for me or to tell me to get out of the way?* My heart was in my mouth. Literally. I looked towards the glove compartment, knowing full well what was hidden inside, his gold-plated iPhone and his fucking finger in a surgical glove.

How that fuck would I explain that.

The nerves and the guilt washed over me like a tidal wave as I innocently continued to indicate, moving onto the inside lane, anticipating my exit. Then the noise I dreaded.

The sirens.

The fucking sirens.

That's it. It's over. Not even twenty-four hours and I've been caught. I pulled over onto the hard shoulder, turned the engine off, lit another cigarette, and smoked it like it was my last.

WEST HAMPSTEAD

I looked straight ahead, with the glare of the police headlights behind, watching the raindrops besiege the windscreen and zig zag down the glass. Smoke engulfed the interior of my Golf and then there came the inevitable tap on the driver's window.

Boy, I was nervous.

This is it. It's over. Freedom is over. Bizarrely, what was playing on the Martin Collin's late-night show at that very moment? Freedom by George Michael. You couldn't make it up.

"Good evening sir. Can I have a look at your driving licence please."

"Evening officer, is there a problem?" I asked, trying to sound as innocent as possible.

"I'd just like to see your driving licence please sir."

"Yes of course," I responded stabbing my cigarette out in the overfilled pull out ashtray beneath the radio, which was now silent.

I opened my wallet and handed over my licence.

Don't ask me to open the glove compartment. Just don't ask me!

"Thank you. I won't be a minute."

As I pressed the switch to close the electric window, I wanted to spark up another cigarette, but I didn't want to appear nervous. I waited, looking out of the rear-view mirror, trying to gage my fate by watching the two policemen in deep conversation, under the interior light in the car.

They're going to nick me. I just know it.

I checked the side mirror again, and after what seemed like an age, the same policeman heaved himself out of the car and approached mine. My nerves were on edge as he came to my side and as the electric window slid down, he asked me to get out of the car.

"Can you come with me please."

I obliged. Of course.

This is it; this is the moment. They're going to handcuff me and throw me into the back of their car.

As I walked towards the rear of the car, getting soaked by the rain, he stopped me.

"Do you see this sir?" He pointed to the rear brake light.

"The brake lights?"

"Yes sir. But also, the right light."

"Oh, I don't tend to look at the rear lights as I drive, I'm afraid."

Why be so flippant, you dick.

"They're both not working."

Is this the reason why they stopped me. It can't be, they're playing with me.

"I must ask you to get these repaired with urgency. It's an offence."

So is murdering someone.

"Of course. I will get them repaired first thing tomorrow morning officer."

Stay calm. Stay calm. You could get away with this.

"Do you have far to go?"

"Just meeting a friend close by, then back to West Hampstead a bit later."

"Okay, but please rectify this problem first thing tomorrow."

"I will. Tomorrow. I promise."

"Good, please make sure you do. Here's your licence and have a safe journey back."

"Thank you officer."

"One more thing sir."

Deja vu, Columbo.

"Get that wiper fixed."

I nodded.

"Make sure you do, for your own safety."

"I will, first thing."

"Goodnight sir."

"Goodnight."

As he handed over my driving licence, I momentarily closed my eyes with relief and walked back to my car with my heart thundering as the rain continued to hammer down. Closing the driver's door, I sat back, closed my eyes and drew a breath. It was then, that I thanked God, out loud. It was the first time, for a very long time, that I've done that. With the sound of the police car passing me as I sat stationary, head down and with trembling wet hands, that I then wiped dry onto my jeans, I pulled a cigarette out of the packet, placed it in my mouth and lit the damn thing.

As I smoked in silence, I could actually feel my heart thrusting against my ribcage.

But then I was disturbed, by the ping of the phone.

Where the hell are you?

Clocking the time on the dashboard, it was a few minutes after ten, and I knew I had to dash.

I'm just getting off the M4. I was stopped by the police.

I started the engine, indicated and turned off at junction four.

Ping.

What, and they let you go?

Yeah, they did you fuck whit of an arsehole. Okay, I didn't reply with that, but boy, I was tempted.

Yep. I'll be there soon.

Ping.

You'd better be.

I took a right and then a sharp left and spotted his blacked-out Range Rover on the layby as suggested by him. I also spotted two other people inside.

My phone pinged again.

Get in the car, bring the phone and finger.

I pulled them out of the glove compartment, tucked them inside my jacket and walked over to the car, with the rain was still pelting down.

As I approached, a bald man, twice my size in both height and width, clambered out of the driver's passenger door.

"Get in," he spat.

I did as I was told, and as I climbed in, I spotted an identical looking man, sitting with his arm on the door rest, looking straight in my direction. As I sat beside him, the other guy came in from the damp and shuffled next to me.

THE KRAYS

"**LET** *me* introduce you to Ronnie and Reggie. That's right. Named after the Krays. Their parents were big fans."

Really, you don't say.

"So, tell me, you got stopped by the Old Bill then?"

"Yeah, I thought that was it, thought I'd be handcuffed, the lot, but it was just my rear lights."

"What, not working?"

"Yeah."

"Well with the money you earned, you could buy a fucking new car. You need one." The wannabe Kray twins beside me let out a snigger in unison.

"I may just do that once this murder business has died down," I replied flippantly.

"Oh, a comedian now are we?"

"Not really, just trying to make light of the situation."

"Light? You've just committed a big sin son."

"Tell me about."

"Anyway, where's the phone and the finger."

I pulled out both items from my jacket and passed them to him.

"You know, I didn't think you had it in you. You surprised me."

"Believe me, I didn't think I had it in me either. But you do things for money don't you."

"Well son, money does make the world go round. It gives you power. And I have plenty of both."

"You do Mr Maddox, power and money," a grovelling meat head to my right agreed.

"Shut up," Mad Dog demanded.

"Yes, sorry Mr Maddox," the geezer on my right grovelled.

"But, you," he continued, turning around, looking straight at me, pointing the cut off finger in my face. "You have neither."

Cheers for the reminder.

"Tell me about it."

"I'll tell you about it. I'll tell you that the fucking police came to see me yesterday."

"Really?"

"Yes, really. Standard fucking procedure though. Well, I am the father-in-law of the deceased after all. They wanted to know if I had any idea why my son-in-law was murdered or who did it. If he had any enemies that I knew of, apart from me that is, the bastard."

"Did you mention me?"

"Course not. What do you think I am, some sort of grass?"

I felt movement either side with the Kray Twins inching in either side of me, squashing me, like a clamp, ready to squeeze the life out of me.

"No, no, of course not."

"Correct answer. Anyway, it's your lucky day, or night, as it happens. Of course, I didn't put you in the frame, I'm not like that, you did me a favour."

"Glad I could help."

"Well, at least you didn't get nicked on the way here, and you'll be pleased to know, that you're going to be leaving here without a bruise on that pretty little face of yours."

Just then the boys either side of me, moved away. I also felt my phone vibrate in my jacket pocket. It must be Lisa.

"So, what do I do with this, just put the tip of his finger on this button?"

I leant forward, as he showed me the phone and finger.

"Yes, simple as that."

"Nice phone, he had. All gold, real at that. Do you know who paid for this?"

"No idea." *But I did.*

"Me. Yes, me. I paid for everything, and that bastard stole from me. And not just my precious daughter."

"Is that why you wanted him killed?"

"Not just that, but don't say that word in the car."

"Fine, I won't."

"There were many reasons why I wanted him, you know, to disappear, but that's not for you to know, it's got nothing to do with you."

"Okay, fine with me," I replied shrugging my shoulders.

Anyway. So, I put his fingertip here, yeah?"

"Yes."

"Good. Before I switch it on though, I need to put a device on it to make it untraceable, like your phone, then I'll see what the dead son of a bitch has been up to. Also, do you still have my daughter's number?"

"Yes."

"Good."

"Why?"

"Never question me son. Never."

I looked around at Bill and Ben beside me. They nodded with a smug look on their ugly pale fat faces, that I really wanted to smack.

"I want you to call her."

"Why?"

"Don't question me, I've told you."

"Sorry, but why, when?"

"Don't question me I said. I want you to call her after the wake."

"Why?"

"You and your fucking questions. I'll tell you at the wake."

"When's that then?"

"Jesus, all these questions. In a week or so. I'll confirm where and when once I know. Just lay low until I contact you, don't go anywhere. Fade away."

"Why?"

"Fuck, you are new at this, it's like being at fucking nursery."

At that moment, Bill and Ben chuckled like infants.

"Shut up you two."

"Yes boss," they replied in unison, like naughty school children.

"Because son, they will need to do an autopsy on the body."

"Oh, I see."

"I hope you do. So, as I've said, lay low, stay in your flat, work on your book but keep a low profile and don't do anything to draw attention to yourself."

"What happens if I do?"

"That's your problem son. Just don't mention me, okay?"

"Of course not. Like you, I'm no grass."

"Good, but if you do, just don't have a shower in prison. If you know what I mean."

I did and I nodded.

"Also, at the wake, I'll introduce you to her, my daughter, so she knows who you are. And then you can phone her."

"But why?"

"I mean it, stop asking fucking questions."

"Okay, okay, you're the boss."

"You better believe it. Don't fucking forget it. Right, that's it. You can fuck off now."

"Okay."

"One more thing."

Columbo again.

"I'm a man of my word. I'll give you the rest of the money after the funeral at the wake."

"Sure, I know you are, thanks."

"Safe journey home then. Don't get nicked."

"I'll try not to."

I leapt out of the hundred grand vehicle, with a little spring in my step knowing that I'd survived my third encounter with Mad Dog without a scratch, as I paced towards my hundred pound heap of metal. Sitting behind the steering wheel, watching them drive off and disappear around a bend in the narrow lane, I pulled my phone out. I was right, it was Lisa.

Hey baby, hope you're okay. Just thought I'd say hello. Having fun with girls. See you tomorrow. Love you L xx

I replied, lit up a cig and started to make the journey home, praying I wouldn't get stopped again.

SKY NEWS

IT was just before midnight when I finally closed the car door, with the rain receding back to a slight drizzle. Thankfully I hadn't been stopped again. I looked around, permanently dreading the moment when my collar might be felt by the Old Bill or loan sharks, as I made my way to my flat. I'd managed to park in one of the side roads off West End Lane, about a five-minute walk away, not too close to home.

Once upstairs, having locked the flat door, I felt safe. Well, as safe as I could be under the circumstances. I went into the kitchen, cracked open the Jack Daniels, poured myself a decent measure and added a couple of ice cubes from the freezer. Leaving the ice to mingle with the liquor, I went into the bedroom and **opened the bedside drawer. I pulled out the bag of weed, along with the king size papers, having decided that a joint would complement the drink nicely.**

Drink. Joint. Me.

Who said three's a crowd?

The first hit of the spliff, along with a gulp of the Jack Daniels put me in a more relaxed mood as I went into the living room and clicked the television on. Flicking through the channels, I stopped at Sky News. News about train delays, tickets prices and politicians were being featured, until the story I was nervously waiting for.

My story.

The report by Martin Brunt featured exactly where the murder had taken place, with images of the street, a few bunches of flowers where he'd died, and interviews with a couple of residents who said they'd been there that night. One of them was the sick bastard who'd taken a photo of the body. But there was still no mention of who the victim was, just that he was married and in his mid-thirties.

I wondered if that bloke who had taken the photo had put anything on Twitter. I went over to the table, beside the window, rain bouncing off the pane of glass, with a heavy wind following. I googled Twitter, as I didn't want to go directly from my Twitter account and searched anything to do with Kensington, murder and Fawcett Street. The timeline was pretty full, mainly from the news accounts, but then I came across an image.

He had put the photo of the body on Twitter with the hashtag #KensingtonMurder. It had over three hundred and fifty retweets and one hundred and fifty likes. I scrolled down to look at the comments. Most of them saying what a sick bastard he was for uploading the photo, or RIP to the victim. I wondered if I should retweet, or would I be in the same category as him. A sick bastard.

But I was more than that. I was a murdering bastard. This was my handywork.

I decided against it, just in case the police, who had also tweeted about the murder, asked for any information from everyone who interacted with the tweet. Pouring myself another Jack Daniels and rolling a joint, I went into word and retrieved my book. I added what had happened tonight with the police, Mad Dog Maddox, the Kray Twins and going onto Twitter, well the Americanised version anyway. Another two thousand and fifty words added to the story. I'll email my editor that tomorrow. Then my phoned pinged, it was Lisa.

Hey baby, how was your evening? I'm a bit sozzled and tired. Got to be up again at six, so going to bed. Love you. Sleep well honey L xx

I replied sending my love and wished her sweet dreams. I also stated that I really needed to finish the book as I was under pressure from my editor, so I said that I'd be holed up in the flat writing for the next few days, maybe a week, but really, I was hiding from the police and the outside world.

Then I checked my emails and coincidently, one was from my editor.

WOW. Where did you get this from? It's brilliant. Had me on the edge of my seat. Even though the main character murdered someone, the reader, or me at least, sort of took a shine to him. I love it and can't wait to read the rest. Hurry up, let's get this beauty published. AWESOME.

107

I replied saying that I'd written some more, and once I'd reread it, I'd be emailing that over too.

Collapsing on to the sofa, blowing out the final wisp of the joint as I did so, I went over the events on the evening of the murder. Did I leave any evidence? Did I fuck up in some way? The only thing I could think of was the plaster. I lifted my top and looked down towards my abdomen. The cut was still visible, but without any trace of blood. That's the only thing, if they found the plaster. But as Mad Dog said, I'm clean, I'm invisible to the police, my DNA isn't on any database, they haven't got anything on me, that's why he chose me.

BREAKFAST TV

THE ping of my mobile woke me. Bleary eyed. I checked the time. Seven fifteen. It was a message from Lisa.

Morning handsome, I understand that you want to get the book finished, you do what you need to do. I'll miss you but get that book written. I'm at work now, talk to you later, happy writing L xx

My back was dead stiff as I massaged my face into life. I'd fallen asleep on the sofa, not for the first time, with a full ashtray and empty glass side by side on the wooden floor. Full of guilt, I replied to Lisa thanking her for her understanding about the book, as the morning daylight peeked into the living room through the Venetian blinds, highlighting the dust motes and stale smoke that hung in the air. As I lay on the sofa, dropping my right arm to the floor, I fumbled for my cigarettes. Picking up the packet, along with the lighter, I lit one. One of the first of many today. As I drew in the smoke from my first drag, I thought about what lay ahead, thinking, will the writing be on the wall. Will I make the wake whenever it is, or will the Old Bill come knocking on my door? I fully expected them to. I didn't know what to do. Hide away within these four walls or go and get lost in London somewhere.

The flat was quiet without a sound coming from the TV or radio. I didn't want to watch breakfast TV with the annoyingly effervescent early morning presenters, or listen to the news, and I definitely wasn't in the mood for music. I stabbed out the end of the cigarette and sat up as I did so. Feeling thirsty I went into the kitchen to make a coffee. Pouring myself a black one, I had no choice, there wasn't any milk, I decided to add a drop or two of Jack Daniels. I took a few sips and went into the bedroom. Opening the draw, lifting the envelope out, full of cash, I tipped the contents onto the unmade bed. I counted. Six thousand pounds, with another ten at the wake. Sixteen thousand pounds. I could go away, escape abroad. Start a new life. I had no ties here, apart from Lisa, and I could write my book from anywhere in the world.

As I thought about my next move, there was a buzz on the entry phone. I froze, terrified, surely the police couldn't have tracked me down already? Seconds later, I hurriedly bundled the fifty-pound notes back into the envelope. There was another buzz. A prolonged one this time. Peeping out of the window, so as not to be seen, I spotted a white van half parked on the kerb and road with its hazards on, holding up cars who were hooting and trying to negotiate around it. Was it the loan sharks wanting to break my legs?

I moved away and crouched down. *Bloody knee.*

West End Lane was always busy at this time of the morning. People going to work and on the school run. There was another buzz on the intercom. What should I do, go down, let them in, or what? I was nervous, undecided.

Holding my breath, I waited for another buzz. But it didn't follow. Again, I peeped out of the window and noticed the van driving away, a vehicle or two ahead on West End Lane. I closed my eyes with relief and decided to go downstairs to see if anything had been left for me. It had. A white card, size of a postcard, looking ominous against the red tiled terracotta floor and addressed to me. It wasn't the sharks but bailiffs, stating that they had taken over the debt, asking me to call them urgently, within twenty four hours about the outstanding council tax I owed. Five months' worth, amounting to around seven hundred and fifty quid. *I can pay that.* I smiled with relief having thought initially it was the police or the loan sharks. I called the bailiffs straight away and arranged for them to come back the next day, when, with a degree of satisfaction, I was able to clear that particular debt in one hit. My £10k was now £5k. I've never looked forward to going to a wake before but I was eager to claim the rest of my fee.

KENSINGTON

IT's been a week since I last saw Lisa. I've hidden in silence, with no TV or radio, just writing within these four walls. Only phone calls, messages and emails from Lisa, Mad Dog and my editor for company, and only stepping outside every other day for cigarettes, alcohol, food and milk. I'd managed to write another twenty five thousand words which I'd already emailed to my number one fan, my editor.

One of the many messages from Mad Dog was to tell me that the wake of the man I killed was tomorrow afternoon.

With the thought of driving tomorrow, I remembered, the police.

My car. The lights. The bloody wiper.

I reminded myself that I had to take the car into the garage. *Only a week late*. I just couldn't take another chance. I grabbed the keys, ran to my car and drove to the nearest mechanics. Thankfully there was one up the road, just off West End Lane.

"No probs, mate, come back say twelve, twelve-thirty tomorrow, to pick the car up, it'll be done by then."

"You sure, I need to be at a funeral, I mean wake by three in Kensington."

"Yeah, dead sure mate," the guy with a wrench replied, grinning.

Yeah, fucking hilarious.

Arriving back at the flat, I got undressed and had a shower. Once dried and dressed I had another coffee, of course with another drop of Jack Daniels and a cigarette, then my phoned pinged.

Baby, I've forgotten what you look like, can I come over tonight, it's been a week? L xx

Hey beautiful. Yes, come over it's been a while. See you later xx

Just then my company phone sprang to life.

Don't forget, 3 tomorrow. My house, you've got the address.

How could I. It's the wake of the man I killed.

I'll be there.

Of course, I'll be there, especially with ten grand waiting for me. But the thing is, who else would be there?

CHELSEA

"**THANKS** for last night baby. Sorry I zonked out. The wine and being exhausted did it for me," Lisa said as she cuddled up to me in bed.

"That's okay. You were tired anyway after another long shift."

"Tell me about it. I'd better get up, another bloody long day ahead," Lisa replied as she walked over to the window, naked.

"What a beautiful morning it is," she added, peeking through the blinds at the outside world.

"Yes, what a beautiful sight indeed."

"Oh, stop it," she giggled, blushing slightly as she covered herself with both arms.

"Also, baby, thanks for walking me to the station."

"That's okay, I would drive you but the cars in the garage."

"I know, it's fine, it's getting late, I'd better get a shower."

The early morning thinly laced frost dusted the pavement and we left a trail of footprints behind us as we made our way to the station. Autumn leaves of red, yellow, and green coloured the muddy grassless verge as we walked hand in hand.

"So, what are you up to today?" Lisa enquired.

What am I up to today? Well, collecting the car from the garage, driving across London to the wake of a man I killed and picking up another ten thousand pounds for doing so, so all in all, not a lot.

"I'm picking up the car from the garage as you know, then I'm going back to continue working on the book."

"How's it going?"

"Great. It was worth me being holed up in the flat, I emailed my editor twenty five thousand words yesterday."

"Wow, that's amazing and what did she say?"

"She loves it. She replied saying it was AWESOME, you know Americans, and asking where I plucked the story from."

"So, where did you pluck the story from?"

"Just my own thoughts."

"Dark ones I'm sure."

"You could say that."

"But she loved it then?" she asked with a surprised tone.

"Yes, don't sound so surprised."

"I'm not, but you keep telling me how you have writer's block and how demanding she is and......"

"I know. I know. I'm joking. Sorry. But I've been on a roll recently, and she loves it, she's my number one fan."

"That's wonderful news. I'm so proud of you baby."

You wouldn't be if you knew how and where I plucked the story from.

"Thank you, baby."

"Oh, and by the way, I'm your number one fan baby."

"I know you are baby."

"Right, better go, my train leaves in one minute, you go back and carry on writing this 'AWESOME' book and I'll message you at lunchtime."

"Okay, have a good morning."

"Chance will be a fine thing, love you baby."

We kissed goodbye and off she went to save the world. Well, at least perhaps a few patients. I spotted the Metro stand, half full of papers. I couldn't resist grabbing a copy, seeing if my murder was still being featured. Turning the first few pages, I came to my story on page seven.

*Police are still searching for the killer of the man found dead in a Kensington street. The victim, who has been identified as Matthew James, had a finger missing and **his gold-plated mobile phone had been stolen. He** was thirty-six*

116

and married. Police are still asking for anyone with information to come forward.

Walking back to my flat I felt vulnerable. Hand in hand with Lisa I'd felt safe, or as safe as I'll ever be. It was like she was my protector. But she didn't know what she was protecting.

Closing the paper, as I opened the door, I felt safe again as I shut the door behind me. *His finger and his phone. You know who's got that. Mad fucking Dog.* I expected a message on the company phone to follow any second. Any minute. He must have read the paper, surely, he must. Maybe he's too busy with the funeral preparations and final details. Or even consoling his daughter.

Climbing the stairs to my flat, I wandered into the bedroom. *Suit. Black suit. I need my suit.* Pulling out my one and only suit from the wardrobe, along with my solitary tie, looking sad and lonely, I laid them on the bed next to my slightly creased white shirt. *It's fine, the jacket will cover the creases.* I went into the kitchen, switched the kettle on, then into the lounge, opened up my laptop, put in my password and started to write about the past twenty-four hours. Two and a half hours, and three cups of Jack Daniel's enhanced coffee later, I'd produced another two thousand, seven hundred and ninety-five words. I sent my latest work off to my editor.

My mood swung like a pendulum, like a ticking time bomb upon my shoulders. One minute I was on a high, especially after sending my work in progress to my editor,

117

then as I got dressed for the wake of the man I'd murdered, my mood sank, buried in a time of despair. Looking in the mirror as I tied a Windsor, pushing the knot to the buttoned-up collar, sweat began to tighten around my neckline.

What if the police are at the wake as well as the funeral? What if they spot me? What if they start to ask questions? Could I cope? I was petrified, completely out of my depth, but I had to go to the wake. I had another ten grand to pick up. That doesn't happen every day of the week, believe me.

But nor does murdering someone.

Giving myself one last final check in the mirror, I went into the kitchen and poured myself a little hit of Jack Daniels. No ice this time. Glass in hand, I walked around the flat, like it would be my last time. *Please don't let it be the last time. Please God don't let the police be there.* I sparked a cigarette. I could have really done with a joint, but I thought I'd save that till later. If in fact there would be a later. And anyway, I'm driving. Yes, I was having a drink but I can cope with that. A couple of small ones wouldn't put me over the limit. I ambled over to the window and looked at the view, again as though it was for the very last time. It was a great view, overlooking the rooftops of London. This is why I pay top money. But who has time to stand looking out at the view all day? Finishing off the cigarette at the same time as the Jack Daniels, it was time to go. Picking up both phones, along with the cigarettes, I closed the door, went downstairs, out the door, and paced the short walk to the mechanics up the road. Suited and booted marching along West End Lane, the company phone vibrated.

The filth, they're here. As I said, don't come to the funeral. We'll talk at the wake. The bastards aren't invited to that.

I replied as I entered the garage at twelve-thirty, and as promised the car was ready. I paid in cash, drove out the forecourt and made my way, across London to his house in Chelsea.

KINGS ROAD

GETTING into the car, sparking up yet another cigarette, I negotiated the horrific afternoon traffic, mainly clogged up with yummy mummy's picking up their spoilt brats from private schools in their expensive four-by-fours. Driving along the Kings Road, I felt completely inadequate in my battered twenty-year-old Golf, but having turned left into Ashburnham Road, I managed to reverse into a tight spot between a Porsche and a BMW. Just like Fawcett Street a mile or so away, this road oozed wealth.

Paying for a ticket to park, I placed it on the dashboard and slowly walked towards an imposing and very handsome four-story Georgian style property. Before I'd even lifted my arm to knock on the door, with the predictable black lion door knocker, Mad Dog appeared, and without saying a word, ushered me back down the four mosaic tiled steps to take me for a wander along the leafy road back in the direction of the infamous Kings Road.

"So, you're here then."

"It seems like it."

"What I mean is fuck features, you didn't get pulled over by the Old Bill on the way here."

"I was at the grounds for a few minutes, you know, just to show my respects, but don't worry I didn't get out of my car and I was well hidden. I did see them but they definitely didn't see me because I left before they did, so I'm here, aren't I."

"I told you not to go for fuck's sake."

"I didn't get seen alright."

"I fucking hope not. Anyway, just thought I could save myself ten grand you know, but as you're here, and as I promised, this is for you."

He pulled out a fat brown envelope from inside his tailored single-breasted black suit and handed it over in broad daylight on one of London's wealthiest roads.

Quite fitting really.

As before, I didn't count it. I wanted to drive back home with my fingers intact. As I placed the envelope inside my ill-fitting, untailored suit, he took me by complete surprise with his next comment.

"My daughter. She thinks it's me."

"What? What do you mean?"

"She thinks I murdered her bastard of a husband."

"Well, she isn't wrong really is she."

"Don't be fucking cheeky. I'm not in the mood."

"Sorry, but……"

"No buts, I didn't pull the knife on him, you did. You stabbed him, you plunged the knife into his body."

"Maybe so, but you called the shots."

"Look pal, now you have the money, don't fucking test me."

"I'm not. Okay. I'm sorry. So, she thinks it's you?"

"Yes, me, are you fucking deaf?"

"Of course not, but why does she think that?"

"Because she knew how much I detested him."

"So, why would she think you killed him?"

"History."

"But I don't know anything about that."

"And you're not going to. It's nothing to do with you."

"Okay, fair enough. I was only trying to help."

"Help. You? How can you help. Who do you think you are? You murdered once. ONCE and now you think you're one of the Kray twins or something."

"No, no, I just thought."

"Well, don't fucking think."

The atmosphere between us, in the West London afternoon air, turned frosty as we crossed the Kings Road.

Stopping the traffic like he owned the place, thumping one or two stationary car bonnets as he passed, he was completely unphased by the drivers swearing at him and honking their horns, using finger language in return as he strolled nonchalantly in their paths.

He didn't give a shit. He was Mad Dog Maddox. He ruled the world. Or so he thought.

I lit another cigarette as we walked side by side, knowing that any minute his personality can change like the bitter wind that was giving me the chills.

And it did.

"You know, you can help," he announced in a friendly manner.

"How?"

"Well, you remember last week, when you nearly got pulled over?"

"How can I forget."

"Did you sort the lights out by the way?"

"Yes."

"Good. Anyway, you remember that I wanted you to call my daughter?"

"Yes."

"Well, what I need is, for you to tell my daughter that it wasn't me."

"Me?"

"Fuck, you are fucking deaf. Yes, you."

"But why me, what about, you know, Ronnie and Reggie?"

"Oh, come on, she doesn't talk to Tweedle Dum and Tweedle Dee. She hasn't got time for those two morons. I only have them for their fucking muscle, not their fucking brains, or complete lack of them. But you, you come across as articulate, affable and she likes that."

"But…."

"No, buts, I've told you, you're the one who has to tell her. You're the one who has to tell her it wasn't me."

"But what if she asks who did do it, who killed her husband?"

"She will, of course she will."

"So, what do I tell her?"

"You tell her the truth," he paused, then he continued, "you tell her, it was you."

I nearly choked on the smoke I'd just inhaled from the cigarette.

"What? Me? Oh, come on, you know I can't do that, no way, no fucking way, no chance. No fucking chance."

"Well pal, it's either that, dealing with me, or the Old Bill, who will be knocking on your blue door, before you can book a flight out of this shithole of a country."

"How'd you know it's blue?"

"Oh, come son, be serious," he said chuckling loudly, as he lit up one of his fat cigars. *Probably from Cuba.* "I've been in this game far too fucking long not to get to know all about who I choose to employ, and where they live. Also, your woman, Lisa, yes, Lisa isn't it, yeah, cute girl, very, very cute, I must say. Tidy body and all that. I like that she works in a hospital too, saving lives, helping people and all that, you know. Very commendable. I must say."

"What. You leave her out of this, she doesn't know a fucking thing."

"Well, you do as I say, and I won't have to send Ronnie and Reggie around to pay her and her beautiful three flatmates a visit at their place."

The conversation became taut with the tension in the air escalating as we made our way back to his imposing house and up the steps.

"Look son," he said as he turned to face me at the top of the stairs, "you seem like a nice enough kid to me and I don't want any trouble, I've had far too much in my life, but if you don't do as I say, well, I'm afraid, Lisa…."

"Yeah, yeah, I get it," I interrupted with a choke in my throat.

"Good, that's settled then," he smirked as he closed the door behind us, to the outside world.

GRIEVING WIFE

HELPING myself to a small Jack Daniels, knowing I had to drive back, I wandered from the luxurious fitted kitchen, which was as big as my entire flat, into the living room, which was even bigger, where family and friends of the deceased were drinking, smoking and chatting.

Just like a fucking party.

In between the gathered mourners, I spotted Jennifer across the room, in floods of tears, dressed head to toe in black, highlighting her blond hair. She stood between Mad Dog and a woman who I assume was her mother. He attempted to put an arm around her, to comfort her, but she pushed him away without any hesitation and that triggered in me a sense of mild alarm. She leaned to her left, towards her mother, clearly a woman of strength, who stabilised her with a supporting arm around her daughters slim waist, as Jennifer's head was buried in the arc of her mother's neck, burying the cries of her loss.

127

I felt responsible for her pain, of course I did. I was responsible. I'd murdered her husband, but it had to be done. That is what I was told.

The grieving wife will see reason one day, I hope.

"Oh, there he is, come over here son." I heard his softer, more welcoming, but pretend voice within the crowd of people, arm raised, his fingers beckoning me over to him.

I acknowledged and did as he asked, with an equally pretend, gracious nod and smile.

"Jennifer," he called, trying to gain her attention, as he led me to his daughter, who was now sitting down next to her mother, sipping a glass of wine, facing the room, as grey clouds gathered behind them through the vast bay window.

"This is the guy I was talking to you about." He put his right hand on my shoulder, with his left clasping a tumbler of whisky and a trademark cigar smoking in the corner of his mouth.

"I'm so sorry for your loss," I empathised as I placed my empty glass on the windowsill behind them, held her right hand in mine and covered it with my left.

"Thank you," she responded, as she stared in my direction with her melancholy eyes, reminding me of the crime I had committed.

"And to you too," I said, turning to my right to her mother. It was immediately evident from where Jennifer inherited her attractive features.

"Mum, I need a refill, do you want a top up?"

"Yes darling, thank you."

"Looks like you could do with one too," she uttered to me, noticing my empty glass as I retrieved it from the windowsill.

"Just a tiny one as I have to drive back."

"Of course, you don't mind, do you?" she asked, as she looped her arm around mine.

"No, not at all.."

"I know we've just been introduced but I just feel a bit shaky," she added.

"It's understandable under the circumstances, go ahead," I responded, feeling incredibly guilty, arm in arm with the wife of the man I'd murdered, who's portrait was on show above the inglenook fireplace. I swear his eyes were following me. I was all too aware that her right elbow was mere inches away from the blood money in the envelope in my inside jacket pocket.

As we passed that gathering of people and headed into the kitchen, out of the corner of my eye, I spotted Mad Dog, nodding agreeably, raising his glass to me as he did so.

"Here, let me do this." I picked up the bottle of wine to uncork it.

"No need, we have waiters to do that."

"It's fine, they're busy, I'll do it, I don't mind."

"Thank you, that's very kind."

"It's the least I can do, believe me."

"So, I've not seen you around here before, why's that?" she questioned as I finally, after a bit of a battle, uncorked the bottle, poured the wine into two glasses, and handed her one.

"Thank you."

"You're welcome."

She took a sip, then continued.

"Have you been to this house before?"

"No, first time and a beautiful house it is too."

"I thought so."

"What do you mean?"

"Well, you really don't seem to be the usual sort of individual that visits."

"Really?"

"Yes, look around you, look at them all, nothing but lowlife money grabbing thugs, but after hearing about you, my first impression is the complete opposite."

"Thanks, but you really don't know me."

"I have great intuition, trust me."

"And that's what may I ask?"

"That you are nothing like these lowlifes or my bastard of a stepfather."

You won't be thinking that after I've told you that I murdered your husband.

Pouring myself another drink, I paused, looked at her and queried.

"Stepfather?"

"Yes, stepfather."

"I didn't know."

"Why would you. I'm sure he's enchanted you with tales of what a great father he is to me and what an amazing husband he is to my mum, but he's nothing of the sort, the bastard."

Sipping the JD, I was rather taken aback.

"But what about your real father?" I thought about what I'd said. "Sorry, that's inconsiderate of me, I shouldn't have asked, forgive me."

She looked at me. Her grieving eyes telling the story.

"Look. It's alright, you weren't to know. My mum adores him for some reason," she chortled, "well, I know the reason, he drapes her in diamonds and pearls. All the luxury trappings of blood money, unlike my real father. He didn't have the same mentality as him, believe me, but he paid the price."

Blood money!

"What do you mean, **paid the price**?"

"Well he, my father, I mean, I don't know, he went missing shortly after I got married. Not a phone call, not a letter. No communication at all, not a word."

"But your mother, what does she think?"

"She doesn't talk about it, I've tried to discuss dad with her, believe me, but I know my stepdad is involved somehow, I just know it. Oh God. I can't. I just can't talk here. This room, this bloody house has eyes and ears."

I looked at her with a raised eyebrow, as we walked back from the kitchen into the living room. Her arm again looped into mine as I carried her mother's glass of Pinot Grigio, and deliberately avoided looking at the portrait to my right, but I felt Mad Dog's eyes following us as I passed the glass to her mother.

"Thank you dear."

I smiled.

"No problem Mrs Maddox."

"Call me Madeline."

"Okay Madeline."

She smiled.

Looking around at the grieving family and friends, I say grieving, it seemed to be more of an excuse for a jolly good piss up. Of course, I knew that the reason they were all here today was because of me. ME. This. Today. It was all my doing.

I killed the poor bastard.

Feeling awkward and with overwhelming remorse washing over me, I made an excuse to leave.

"I have to dash I'm afraid, and again, I'm very sorry for your loss."

"Off so soon?" Jennifer replied.

"Yes. I'm in the middle of writing a book, its overdue and my editor in America is banging on my door. Well, not literally obviously."

"Maybe she's not the only person who will be banging on your door," Mad Dog added in my ear, *where did he come from?* His cigar and whisky breath threat, inches from my face. I looked at him and offered a glare.

He in turn replicated with a menacing look that sent chills down my spine.

"Oh, an author, hear that darling."

"Yes mother."

"How interesting. I love reading, and I've always wanted to write," Madeline replied.

"So, what are you writing about?" Jennifer enquired.

"It's set in America. New York to be precise, about a writer, bit of a thriller, very dark, and a murder thrown in." Too late I realised what I'd said. *You idiot.* "I'm so sorry, really I am, I didn't mean to be so insensitive."

"That's okay, don't worry, it's fine. It's fine. You must tell me more about it some time."

"Yes, you must," Mad Dog barked.

"Give him your number sweetheart, he can call you, once this is over."

"THIS. THIS!" she bellowed straight back, creating a sudden silence in the room, apart from a few whispers, "this is Matthew's funeral for God's sake, my husband's funeral, not one of your gangster reunions."

"Darling, don't talk to your father like that," Madeline added.

"He's not my sodding father, mum," she cut back through gritted teeth.

Then there was nothing. Not a sound in the room. All eyes were staring in our direction. I quickly threw back the remaining few drops of the Jack Daniels.

"You're upset love, I understand," he responded in a very patronising way.

"You'll never understand, and don't call me love. I'm not one of your bloody call girls," she reacted as he looked at her with one of his menacing glares, and as quick as a flash with a smile, turned to look at his wife, Madeline.

"Look. I really have to go, I have a deadline to finish the book, I'm sorry."

"Fine, I'll see you out," Mad Dog instructed.

"No, no you won't. I will, you stay here and be with your wife," Jennifer responded, in an equally demanding manner.

"Let her, just let her show him out," her mother insisted.

134

"Fine, okay, no problem," he said, giving in, holding his hands up before him, backing out of the way.

"Goodbye Madeline and again, my condolences."

"Thank you and hope to see you soon."

"I'll be in touch," Mad Dog added, pointing towards me, which I purposely ignored as Jennifer ushered me into the hallway.

"I'm, I'm so sorry about that, really, it was so uncalled for," she apologised as she pulled the front door to behind her.

"No need to be sorry," I responded as we stood on the step.

"But I am sorry, especially on a day like today. He really infuriates me sometimes, you know. In fact, most of the time. It's just that I have no one to talk too. My friends, one by one have deserted me, now my husband has gone, and my mum, well...."

"I understand. But, but what did you mean about your father paying the price?"

She leaned in close to me.

"I can't talk here, like I said, eyes and ears," she whispered.

"I understand, don't worry."

"It's just that...."

"Oh, you still here then?"

It was Mad Dog.

"It looks like it, but I'm leaving now."

"Safe journey home then. Until tomorrow," he replied as his shadowy figure disappeared behind the partially closed door, leaving a trail of cigar smoke that quickly vanished into the late afternoon air.

"Tomorrow?" Jennifer responded.

"Figure of speech I guess," I replied.

"Yes, he's good at that. Too good."

"So, if you want to meet up for a coffee and talk?"

"Would you?"

"Of course."

"You're not just saying that because he did?"

"No, not at all."

"You don't think it's awful of me, you know, having just buried my husband?"

"Of course not. You're grieving and need someone away from the family to talk to."

"That's very understanding of you."

"I do understand. I lost both my parents in a car accident and I had no one to turn to, to talk to. No brothers, sisters, no one."

"That's awful. I'm so sorry to hear that."

"Thank you. It's fine. It happened a long time ago."

"But still…."

"I know. You never get over it. You never get over losing your parents."

"I know. My father. Look, I'd better go back inside."

"Of course. So, I'll see you soon."

"Yes, that would be great. Do you want to put my number in to your phone?" she suggested.

"Good idea." I punched the number into my phone as she dictated it. "Thank you. It's cold, you'd better get back, and so should I, rush hour traffic and all that."

"Yes, okay, thank you so much for coming," she said as she placed a hand on my arm. "I'm sure that Matthew, my husband," she paused as she wiped a tear from her bloodshot eyes, "would have liked you."

I'm not so sure.

"I'm sure he was a good man."

"Good? Not the word I would use. He had his moments, believe me. Some of the things he did, were, well…." her voice trailed off as she looked straight into my eyes and then continued.

"Just plain awful. I haven't told anybody, not a soul, I just can't."

Once she said that, any guilt I felt about his murder was dead and buried.

"Look as I've said, I'm here if you'd like to get things off your chest."

"That's kind. I may, no, I will take you up on that."

"Do so. I'd better dash. Take care and I'll call you."

"Thank you. Safe journey home."

"Thanks."

Climbing into the car, inserting the keys into the ignition, I lit up another cigarette. Closing my eyes, I felt the smoke travel down towards my lungs. I thought about what had just happened. I even spoke out loud because it just seemed ridiculous.

I'm going to meet for coffee the wife of the man I murdered. She wants to know about the book I'm writing, which in reality, is about her stepfather paying me twenty thousand pounds to murder her husband.

The vibration of the company phone threw me off my train of thought. It was him.

I hear you're meeting up. Sooner rather than later, like in the next couple of days, okay. You know what to do, tell the truth, otherwise you'll face the consequences.

TOWER OF LONDON

I drove against the traffic, across West London back to North West London, as quickly as I could, with thoughts of Jennifer racing around my mind. I parked the car, and with the fear of being caught, I hurried back to the safety of my flat. It was just after five-thirty with darkness settling. The flat was cold. Fucking freezing. I swapped my jacket for a jumper and hid the second envelope of money with the first underneath the book, in the bedside table drawer. Pouring a much needed double Jack Daniels, I whacked the heating on, sat down, opened my laptop, and with smoke from a newly lit cigarette circling around me, began to tap away on the keyboard, getting down the next few chapters of events that had taken place.

As I did so, I spotted an email from my editor. Clicking it open, it read,

Are you kidding? From absolute zilch to this piece of awesome work. Where were you hiding this beauty? It has me so gripped that I can't wait to read the rest. Hurry up and send the next chapters.

Falling back into the seat, I felt like a writer, an author, for the first very time in months, years, my whole life. But as that miniscule moment of self-gratification vanished and I relayed the storyline in my head, the company phone vibrated on the table next to my laptop.

Jennifer, she likes you.

That's good to know. I replied.

Another ping, but this time it was a message from Lisa.

Hey baby, I'll be with you just after eight, I'll grab a couple of ready meals on the way and a bottle of red. Can't wait to see you. Love you L xx

Messaging her back, I continued to write my apparently awesome piece of work, adding in the wake and Jennifer.

Just then, the company phone pinged again.

I hear you're calling her tomorrow. Do so and meet her the day after. She likes the Tower of London, it's one of her favourite places, meet her there. You tell her then. UNDERSTAND.

Understood. I responded.

It pinged again.

And afterwards you can fuck off with the cash for all I care. But remember, if you don't tell her. LISA……..

Bastard.

I'll do it, don't worry.

Ping.

I'm not worried. LISA........

Fucking bastard.

Closing my laptop with an additional three thousand seven hundred words under my belt, I opened the draw of the desk table and whipped out the small copper tin that housed my new addiction. Pulling out the king size rizlas along with the plastic bag of decreasing weed, there was enough for another three or four joints if I was tight with it. Once rolled, laying on the sofa, I sparked it up as I channel surfed. Catching the tail end of The Simpsons on Channel 4, I flipped over to Sky News to see if there was any news of the murder that I'd committed. Nothing. Thankfully.

GUILTY FEELINGS

*"**WHY** DID you do it? She had nothing to do with this, Lisa was fucking innocent, why did you have to kill her?"*

"Because you didn't tell Jennifer, and I told you what I would do."

"But, but I couldn't, the timing wasn't right. It just wasn't right."

"You had your chance, your one and only chance, and I told you what the consequences would be."

"You bastard, no, no, no, she didn't deserve to die............."

"Baby, baby, wake up, wake up."

"Fuck. What, what?"

"You're talking nonsense again and you're sweating."

"Thank God. Thank God it's just a dream, fuck, that seemed so real."

"What did you dream?"

"Doesn't matter, really, it doesn't, just, just come here baby."

"But what did you mean she didn't deserve to die?"

"I don't know. It was just a dream."

"Bad one at that."

"I know. Just give me a cuddle."

I held Lisa tight. I didn't want to let her go.

"Baby, you sure you're okay, you're squeezing me to death."

A word that was so befitting at that moment. Unfortunately.

"Sorry baby, yes I'm fine. You're here, that's the important thing. What's the time anyway?"

"Just after eight."

She then looked over my shoulder towards the desk.

"What's that?"

"What baby?"

"That, the tin, the copper tin?" she questioned again as she stood and walked over to the desk.

Fuck!

"Oh baby, I thought you gave this shit up years ago?"

"I did, I just needed a boost?"

"A boost, why?"

"Well, it helps me with my writing, imagination and all that. And I'm under pressure to get this book finished."

"I know, but…."

"Look, you caught me, hands up, guilty."

"Yes, it looks like I have."

"And I was sort of celebrating."

"Without me?"

"We'll do that later."

"What are you celebrating anyway?"

"The book."

"What about it?"

"She loves it."

"Who?"

"My editor in New York dummy, she just loves it."

"Oh baby, that's fantastic. You'll be signing copies at Waterstones soon. I just know it."

"Thanks, let's hope so."

"Don't doubt it, you will."

"Fingers crossed."

"Anyway, when am I going to read this bestseller?"

"Ah, you will have the very first copy, signed by yours truly."

"Now, that's worth waiting for baby. I knew you could do it."

"Thanks for showing faith in me."

"Always baby, you know that. Right better get dinner going, well, put it in the microwave. Oh, could you open the wine, I'm drying for a drink."

"Sure, I could do with one as well."

Uncorking the red, which was a lot easier that the white I'd opened at the wake a few hours earlier, I poured two glasses. We chatted in the kitchen, as Lisa pierced the film of the ready meals putting them in the microwave, and I set the table with crockery and cutlery.

"So, how was work today baby?"

"Oh, the usual mayhem in A and E. Sick people who are really sick, and the usual time-wasters, wasting our time and costing the NHS money they haven't got."

"Nothing new there then."

"No. Same shit, different day. Oh, I see they still haven't found who murdered that guy in Kensington."

"Yeah, I know, saw it on the news earlier."

"His poor wife. What she must be going through."

"I know, it's tragic."

"Apparently the funeral was today," Lisa replied.

"Yes, in Chelsea. There were a lot of people at the grounds and then at the wake at the house."

"How do you know, were you there?" she questioned with a smirk on her face.

"Yeah right, it was a proper knees up."

There was a ping that broke the conversation, thankfully not from my company phone, that was next to my laptop in the lounge, but the microwave as the ready meals were ready to be eaten.

"This spag bol is pretty good."

"Yeah, not bad, from M&S, mind you, you'll eat anything now."

"Why do you say that?"

"Munchies," she replied with a beaming smile.

"Yeah, yeah. Thanks for getting it anyway."

"Don't be silly, it's on the way home."

Topping up her glass, Lisa again brought up the subject of my book.

"So, this book, this bestseller, tell me about it."

"You want to know?"

"Of course, baby."

"Well, it's about a struggling author, writing his first book, based in America."

"Oh. It's not about you then?" she replied laughing.

"No baby, as I've said, it's set in America and definitely not about me."

"Carry on baby."

"Well, this author, mid-thirties, who lives in New York, owes money, lots of money, thousands."

"Phew, not like you then."

"Nope. Told you. Can I continue please?"

"Yes, sorry baby."

"It's okay. Well, he's desperate, not just to write his book, but he's in so much debt, up to his eyeballs with rent arrears and other debts, and he needs money fast, and I mean fast. He hasn't got any family, no siblings, his parents are dead, and he has bailiffs and vicious loan sharks banging on his door eager to break his legs. He gets caught up with some bad people, via a friend of a so called friend and is paid a lot of cash, by the head honcho, to murder someone, a member of his family."

"Wow. Thank heavens it's not based on you then."

"I can't kill a spider, never mind a human being."

"Don't I know it, I'm the one who has to take them out of the bath."

"Alright. Alright. Anyway, that's where I'm up to. I did write more today, but I need to reread it."

"Sounds very intriguing and dark baby."

"Thanks, it is. As I said, my editor loves it, she thinks it's AWESOME, as they say over there, so fingers crossed."

"I'm sure it will be a huge worldwide hit."

"Thanks. More wine?" I asked finishing off my meal.

"Absolutely, thanks."

"Leave the washing up to me, fancy a bath and an early night."

"What's all this baby, missed me today?"

"Always miss you baby," I replied with guilty feelings.

"You bring the wine and I'll light some candles."

"I'll roll a joint too, it's good stuff."

"I don't know baby."

"Oh, go on, we're celebrating?"

"Okay then as we're celebrating, but just a little puff."

"Of course baby."

As I crumbled the weed into the tobacco and began to roll a joint, I heard the water rushing from the taps into the bath.

The company phone pinged.

Don't forget tomorrow.

How can I.

I won't, don't worry. I replied.

Don't worry, why do I have to worry. You're the one who has to worry. Lisa, your girlfriend....

I stared at the message. Closed my eyes and covered my face with my hands as my elbows sat on the table.

Fucking bastard.

"Baby, the bath's ready," Lisa hollered from the bathroom.

"Okay, just finishing rolling the joint."

"I'll be in baby."

Without replying to his message, I took the joint, lighter and ashtray into the bathroom to get stoned so I could forget for a while about his latest death threats towards Lisa.

GLUED TOGETHER

"*I* feel so relaxed now baby, I can't have anymore, here you finish it."

Lisa passed me the tail end of the joint as she laid on top of me. Her nipples slightly visible and erect from beneath the water line, with her bum resting on my protruding cock.

"The water's getting colder by the second, shall we get out and get into bed?"

"Absolutely baby," Lisa replied, as we both stepped out of the bath and headed towards the bedroom.

Hearing the water swirl around the plug hole and disappear, I pulled Lisa close to me, as I wrapped the grey towel around us both, staring into her green eyes. Holding her makeup less face with the palms of my hands, as the towel fell onto the bedroom carpet, her mouth opened as my lips touched hers, inviting my tongue. Our tongues twirled around each other. Pulling her closer, my hands gently teased her smooth slim body. Her hands fixed around my waist, her hips pushing against mine.

I felt my cock grow with excitement.

Lisa pulled her mouth from mine, looking at me as she did so. She began kissing my neck, my chest, as she wrapped her right hand around the shaft of my cock. As her tongue teased my nipples, she gradually lowered herself to my naval and knelt before me. She was eye to eye with my erect cock. Her sultry green eyes looked up at me as she began to lick the head with the tip of her tongue, stirring my cock even further into life. Feeling her hot mouth as she took me in, made me grow even harder as I felt the back of her throat with the head of my cock. My hands were around her head, clutching her hair as she rhythmically moved back and forth with my fully erect cock filling her mouth. My eyes closed as her hand rubbed and twisted my shaft as she continued to suck hard. I could've easily exploded right there and then, but I wanted to feel inside her. I pushed Lisa's head against my cock, making her take me fully. She moaned, she squealed. She couldn't breathe. Saliva ran out of her mouth, down her chin and dripped on to her perfectly formed tits and erect nipples.

Releasing my cock from her mouth, I pulled her up towards me and kissed her deep. Just then I heard my phone ping in the living room. It was the familiar but annoying sound of the company phone. Mad fucking Dog Maddox. What timing for him to message me. Ignoring it, I told Lisa to lay on the bed. On her back.

As she did the phone pinged again.

151

Again, I ignored it.

As I was about to kneel down at the end of the bed to tease her clit, the phone didn't just ping, it rang.

Jesus.

"Two seconds baby, sorry."

I ran naked into the living room, holding my erect cock in my right hand.

Checking the phone, BIG BOLD CAPITAL letters appeared.

LISA!!!

Turning the phone off, as this was not the time, I returned to the bedroom to Lisa, who was laid on the bed waiting for me. Her misty eyes followed me as I knelt at the end of the bed, and pulled her by her legs towards me, until my mouth was breathing between them.

She yelped as the tip of my tongue teased her. Peering up at her as I continued to play havoc with her clit, her eyes were closed, her head rotating from side to side. I massaged her breast with one had as my tongue entered her, stirring, full circle, causing a frenzy as she groaned. She moaned again, as I sat on the bed, now with one and then two fingers inside her.

Slowly penetrating her with my fingers, I moved slightly faster, then faster still, as she pulled my cock into her mouth, sucking hard as my fingers were entering her in and out. I felt her body tense up, her eyes rolling back as she chewed on my hard cock.

"I'm cumming," she murmured, her voice muffled.

"Fuck. I'm cumming," she repeated urgently.

She spat out my cock. Pushed me onto my back and saddled me, taking my cock into her hand and guiding me inside her.

"Ohhh," she moaned.

Bouncing up and down on my shaft, and tilting slightly back, she massaged her tits, pinching and squeezing her nipples, her head and hair whipping from side to side. Eyes closed. Riding me like it was the last time. *Which it easily could be.* My hands were tight around her waist, as I pushed her back and forth with my cock deep inside her.

Pulling her off and turning her onto her front, I knelt behind her. Spreading her bum cheeks as I entered her. She whimpered with each thrust of my cock, the pace was quicker, the fucking was harder.

"I'm cumming," she squealed. "I'm cumming, cum with me baby."

Fucking her like there was no tomorrow, like it was for the very last time, I grabbed her hair as I penetrated her fast with my cock deep inside her.

"I want to cum over your tits and face."

"Okay but keep fucking me. I'm nearly, I'm nearly...ooooooooooooo."

Continuing to fuck her as she moaned, with her wetness all over my cock, I was very close to loading her with my own cream.

"Quick turn over. Turn over now."

She turned over on her back with a huge smile. Fuck she was even more beautiful after an orgasm. She was glowing. I knelt beside her face. She took me in her mouth again. Sucking as she played with my balls that were about to explode. I took my cock from her mouth, rubbing my shaft up and down.

"I'm cumming."

"Baby give it to me," she demanded.

"I'm cumming."

"I want to taste you."

Wanking my cock as she cupped and played with my balls in her hands, I released and shot my semen all over her face and tits. It wouldn't stop. I saturated her, as she continued to rub my cock and the head with the tip of her finger. *She knows I like that.* She then took me into her mouth and sucked out every last drop.

Sweat pouring off us, our hearts pounding, we lay side by side holding hands as we took a moment to recover.

"Wow, baby. That was amazing."

"Thanks, I wasn't bad."

"Don't be so conceited," she chuckled as she rolled over and laid on top of me.

We kissed. Our naked bodies glued together from the mixture of sex and sweat. We cradled each other for the next few minutes in silence, like it was meant to be, but then the atmosphere took a turn for the worse.

TIN OF WEED

"Baby!"

"Yes…." I answered, still breathless from our love making, with my arm around her, looking deep into her sea green eyes.

"Can I ask you something?"

"Depends on what you want to ask."

"You won't know unless I ask you."

"That's true. Ask away," I replied as she pulled the duvet from the bottom of the bed to cover us and rolled over to my left side.

"I will," she replied. "Who was that on the phone, I mean earlier, that you had to pull yourself away from me so quickly," she questioned, as she ran her fingers across my chest.

"When?"

"Baby, come on, don't be silly, earlier, when we were about to make love, you sprinted into living room with your cock in your hand, like an Olympic athlete in a relay race."

"Well, it was the size of a baton."

"You wish, now stop mucking around," Lisa demanded as she grabbed a pillow and playfully whacked me around the head with it.

"Stop that," I gestured.

"I won't until you tell me who it was."

"No one. Honest."

She pillowed me again.

"Stop it."

"Then tell me."

"It was no one."

"It's another woman, isn't it?"

"What, oh come on baby."

"Then tell me it's not."

"Baby, I swear on my life it wasn't another woman. I would never have an affair."

"I didn't say anything about an affair."

"Okay, I'm not having sex with anyone apart from you. Okay?"

"Yes. Fine."

"Good."

"Then who was it?"

"Oh, for God's sake. It was no one."

"Look, I'm not stupid."

"I didn't say you were."

There was a pause.

"Why do you have to spoil the moment?"

"Because I need to know what I'm getting myself into."

"What do you mean getting yourself into? Oh, fuck it, I need a joint."

"See, there you go, off again, trying to shy away from my questions."

"No, I just fancy a joint, okay."

"Another one?"

"Yes, another one."

"Fine."

"Be right back."

"Fine."

I jumped out of bed, headed to the lounge, this time without an erection in my hand, to where my tin of weed was sitting next to the company phone. I thought about turning it on to see if any new messages from him had arrived but then thought better of it. I picked up a cigarette and headed back to Lisa. As I re-entered the cluttered bedroom, with much evidence of our passionate love making, I was stopped dead in my tracks, the guilt must have been etched across my face.

"This is rich, for someone who doesn't have a job at the moment, there's a nice tidy sum of cash you've got hidden in here."

"Oh shit."

"Oh, shit indeed."

"Why were you looking in the drawer anyway?"

"Looking for a phone charger, but that's not the point is it?"

She replied, kneeling, her breasts now visible from the fallen duvet, looking priceless as she tipped the envelope with FIFTEEN THOUSAND pounds in fifty pound notes, onto the bedsheet next to her.

"Explain this please, without any of your fucking bullshit."

"Let me roll a joint first."

"What and then you'll tell me?"

"Look, it's nothing,"

"This amount of money is nothing?"

"I meant the phone call, it was just, just business when I received the message before."

"I don't believe you, just business, yeah right, I can tell when you're lying anyway."

"Oh, how's that then?"

"Your mouth is moving."

"Yeah good one. Funny."

"You're not a drug dealer, are you?"

"That's even funnier," I laughed.

"Then what. Where did you get this kind of cash from, and don't tell me it was an advance from the publishers or your editor, because I know that's bullshit, you haven't got a publisher and an editor doesn't pay the author."

I quickly put a joint together and took a long drag. Closing my eyes as I did so, trying to think of what to say next.

"Come on, tell me," she demanded with increasing anger in her tone.

"You don't want to know. Really, you don't."

"Oh yes I do. So, tell me."

"Can we just forget about it please?" I pleaded as I offered her the joint.

She looked at me and then the joint.

"Fuck it, I need something."

Taking a drag, she turned to me, blowing smoke in my direction. "No. Tell me, it's me, Lisa, your girlfriend. Apparently. You can tell me anything. Apparently."

"Please don't put me in this position."

"Look, just tell me, or I'm leaving right now. I don't give a fuck how good the sex was. I'll never see or talk to you again."

"You won't anyway after I tell you what I've done."

"Try me, go on, try me."

"Okay, you really want to know?"

"Yes, of course I do, anyway how bad can it be?"

"It's bad. Very fucking bad."

"Oh Jesus, what have you done, just tell me."

"Okay, you asked for it."

EYES AND EARS

"**WHAT.** What. That bloke in Kensington. The murder that we've talked about?"

"I did warn you."

"You killed that poor man?"

"He wasn't poor actually, he was minted."

"I don't mean wealth you idiot. You know what I mean," she replied punching my chest.

"Stop it. Stop it." I grabbed her wrists to try and calm her down.

"Let go of me, you're hurting me. Let go," she yelled.

"Okay, okay. Sorry, but no more punching."

"Fine. Just let me go."

In silence, and in unison, we both fell back onto the crumpled bed, as the bundles of cash flew in the air momentarily. One minute passed. Then another. Still silent.

Not a word. Not a sound. Apart from Lisa's heartbeat thumping as she lay beside me, speechless and angry.

I broke the silence, as I looked up at the discoloured ceiling.

"I needed the money."

"What?"

"I needed the bloody money."

"I heard what you said. It's always about money. The root of all evil. But murder. Fucking murder. Why the hell didn't you ask me for some money?"

"I didn't want you to think badly of me."

Chocking on the smoke she'd inhaled from the remainder of the spliff which she then crashed out in the ashtray, she shrieked.

"Are you fucking crazy? You thought I would think badly of you for asking me if you could borrow some money but not for murdering someone? You've taken someone's life. Why didn't you ask me?"

"Maybe I am crazy, but, but you're a nurse, and no disrespect, you earn twenty grand a year and I needed that amount now. I haven't got anyone to ask, no family, no friends, and no bank is fucking stupid enough to give me a loan or another credit card."

"But no amount of money is worth killing someone for, for fuck's sake. You killed someone. Jesus Christ," she retorted trembling.

"I know. I know. Believe me, I wish I hadn't done it, I really do, but apparently this guy deserved it. He was a right nasty individual."

"Oh, and you're not now."

"I may be, but his wife told me he was a right bastard."

"His wife told you. You know the wife?"

"I don't want to talk about it anymore."

"Oh, believe me, you're going to talk about it and now. I want the full story or I'm calling the police."

"I need a cigarette."

"You always need a fucking cigarette, in fact, you can light one up for me too."

"But you don't smoke."

"No time like the present to start again, believe me. And bring that bloody phone with you."

Stumbling out of bed, I picked my jeans up from the floor, pulled them on, pushed my hair back away from my face and went into the lounge.

Picking up the pack, lighter and phone, I lit one and turned the phone back on as I made my way back to Lisa in the bedroom.

It pinged and then pinged again.

"Popular tonight, aren't we?"

I ignored her as I lit the cigarette and passed it to her.

She took a pull of the leaves.

"This is the first cigarette I've had since I was a teenager, look what you're doing to me."

"Well, you'd better enjoy it, because it gets worse."

"Worse, how much worse can it get than having a murderer for a boyfriend?"

"I have to meet Jennifer."

"Jennifer? Who the fuck now is Jennifer?"

"The wife of the man I killed."

She gasped.

"Sorry?" Lisa replied exasperated. "Let me get this straight. You're meeting the wife of the man you killed?" she said, emphasising each word.

"Yes."

"When?"

"In the next couple of days. I said I'd message her tomorrow to arrange it."

"Over my dead body."

"That's the reason why I have to meet her."

"What do you mean?"

"Well, the reason I have to meet Jennifer."

"How do you know her anyway?" Lisa interrupted.

I paused.

Shit.

"I went to the funeral, well the wake."

"WHAT?"

"The wake. Okay. I went. Well, I was told to go by him, the guy who keeps messaging me and that's when he gave me the other ten grand."

"Oh, this gets better every fucking second, it really does, but hold on, you lied to me. You said you were here, at home, writing."

"I did write, and to be honest with you, I didn't actually lie."

"I don't know what to believe anymore."

"I'm telling the truth. Believe me."

"Whatever. I need a drink. Do we have any more wine left?"

"No, it's all gone,"

"Shit."

"But I could roll another joint."

"Bet you could, go on, it's better than nothing, and I need something."

Having rolled a joint in record time, I passed it to Lisa.

Having a stoned Lisa was better than a drunk one, considering what I had to tell her.

"Right, okay," she said after taking a few hits of the joint, kneeling on the bed, facing me, holding the white duvet with her right hand, covering her perfect breasts, and surrounded by fifty pound notes.

"Let me get this straight. So, you killed this man, does he have a name by the way?"

"He did, Matthew James."

"Okay, so you killed this guy, Matthew James for money, for the twenty grand, right?" Lisa questioned as she clutched a bundle or two of cash, then threw them in the air.

"Yes, that's right, well fifteen grand now after paying the outstanding rent and council tax," I answered, sitting up, bare chested, my head resting on the pillows behind me.

"Oh, finally paying some bills then, welcome to the real world."

"Thanks, but sometimes, I don't like the real world."

"Who does, but whatever world you're in now, you're well and truly fucked."

"Don't remind me."

"Trust me I will. Anyway, the murder, what was it, because, what, you owe a lot of money?"

"Yes, thousands, to some very fucking nasty people, who keep knocking on my door, wanting to break my legs and do some other damage."

"So, you killed this guy Matthew, to get some cash to get these nasty fuckers off your back?"

167

"Yes."

"Have you done this before. I mean, killed someone, anyone, anybody?"

"Of course not, don't be stupid."

"Stupid! You are calling me stupid? I don't think I'm the stupid one around here."

Okay, sorry. Sorry."

"Then, you went to his funeral, which was today, right?"

"Well, the wake, that's when I picked up the rest of the money, the ten grand."

"Wake, funeral, whatever, and now you're going to meet the wife of the man you killed, for whatever reason?"

"Correct."

"And, what is that reason?"

"Well, the thing is, she thinks that her stepdad, who I actually thought was her real father, killed him. He's the guy who keeps messaging me, the one who paid me the money."

"Jesus Christ. I gathered that. So, let her think that."

"I can't'."

"Why?"

"I just…."

"Hold on. Hold it. How? Why? Why did you get involved, I mean, I know about the need for cash to get these people off your back, but why did he, the dad, stepdad, whoever, ask you, choose you, to kill his son-in-law?"

"Because, a mate, well, not a mate, a mate of a mate, spoke to him, they knew the situation I was in, in that, I was desperate for the cash."

"I know that, I know, but why you. You?"

"Because I've never done this sort of thing before. You know, I'm not on the police radar as he put it. I'm clean, never been arrested."

"Well, there's always a first time, but the first offence is normally like what, stealing from a shop, or doing something petty, not fucking murder."

"I know. God, it's all so fucked up."

"Tell me about it, his son-in-law, his daughter's husband."

"His step-daughter."

"Doesn't matter who, it's still family."

"I know but, also, at the wake when I was speaking to her."

"Who?"

"Jennifer, the wife."

"You were talking to her?"

"Yes, when we were in the kitchen getting a drink."

"What!"

"It's not what you think, it was completely innocent."

"Unlike you then."

"Touché"

"Whatever, go on."

"Well, we were just, I don't know, we somehow ended up in the kitchen."

"Cosy chat then."

"Baby, it wasn't like that, we were at a wake, her husband's for fucks sake, the man I killed. Anyway, that is when she told me he wasn't her real father and also that her real dad went missing."

"Missing?"

"Yes, missing. She was just about to tell me something but then suddenly stopped. She said she couldn't risk talking about it as apparently the house has eyes and ears."

"Eyes and ears?"

"You know, people watching and listening."

"Fuck. What have you got yourself into?"

"I don't know, but something very heavy."

"You don't say. Look, just don't tell her, let her think it was him, her stepdad who killed her husband. It's simple."

"It's not."

"Just tell her that."

"I can't."

"You can. Of course, of course you can."

"I can't. I just fucking can't."

"Why?"

"Because, if I don't tell her it was me who killed her husband, then….."

"Then what?"

"Have another drag of the joint, you'll need it."

"Just fucking tell me," Lisa screamed crumpling up the bedsheet with her left hand.

"Okay but…..."

"Just tell me for God's sake."

"Give me the joint first, just give me the joint, please."

"Fine."

She passed it. Closing my eyes as I took a long deep drag, I counted to ten as I held the smoke within my lungs."

"Tell me NOW," she cried.

"Okay. Okay," I answered releasing the smoke and opening my eyes. "If I don't tell her I killed him, her husband…."

I paused again.

"Yes, I know who you mean, if you don't tell her, then what, tell me, tell me now."

FIFTY SHADES

"**He** will kill you," I quickly replied.

Silence. Like the calm before the storm.

"WHAT. KILL ME. ME. WHY KILL ME?"

There's the storm.

"Because you're my girlfriend."

She was stunned. Motionless. Tears began to roll down her stunned face.

"Please don't cry baby. Please," I pleaded as I reached for her.

"Please don't cry, you say. Don't cry. Don't, don't fucking touch me. Get the fuck off me," she bellowed, flogging me with her flaying arms and hands, the bedsheet falling from her naked body.

"How do I know you won't actually kill me?"

"Oh, come on babe, I love you and you know, I'm not a murderer."

"Really, you're not a murderer. What have you done then?"

"I know, but."

"But what? I haven't killed anyone. And now I'm the hunted," she sobbed, pulling back the bedsheet to cover her nakedness.

"You're not. I'll make sure nothing, nothing ever happens to you."

"That's the least you can do. Jesus. You couldn't make this up."

"I know, so that's why I have to tell her when I see her."

"And if you don't?"

"Let's not think about that."

"Let's not think about that, what are you talking about. You said he will kill me if you don't tell her it was you. Anyway, how can I believe that's the truth?"

"The messages. On the phone."

"Let's see, give me your phone."

"No."

"Give me your damn phone," she yelled snatching the phone from me and beginning to scroll down the messages.

"You're kidding me. He sent you one just before we made love."

"Yes, he did. See it wasn't a woman."

"I can see that. Oh. Oh, I see now. No wonder you were on form. No wonder you were at the top of your game."

I smiled to myself when she said that.

"Like it would be the last time we'll make love, because, what, I'll be dead."

"No, don't be stupid."

"Stop calling me stupid."

"Sorry."

"Is that all you can say, sorry. Jesus, this is insane."

"I know."

"You could write a book about this."

"Well, funny you should say that."

"There's nothing funny about it at all," she paused, I could see her mind working, then she continued, "hold on. What do you mean? Oh my God, you're not. You're not tell me you're not?" she queried.

"Yes, I am."

"What, the book you've been writing. The book that your editor in New fucking York has said is fucking awesome is in fact what you've done and are doing?"

"Yeah."

"Does she know that the book is in fact a true story of a murder, that you, the author has committed?"

"No."

"She might find out and stop any further editing, or even call the police."

"There's no chance, she's thousands of miles away, and it's set in Manhattan, not London, so she won't have a clue."

"But what about your mate, her son."

"He won't put two and two together. Anyway, he's been travelling around Asia for the past year and will be for next couple."

"OH. MY. FUCKING. GOD," she reacted, sitting on the bed, now with her legs against her chest, her arms wrapped around them. She continued.

"I should have known when you were telling me earlier about the book. It makes sense now. The author, no parents, no siblings. No money. God, I'm stupid."

"You're not stupid."

"Is this going to be in it?"

"Yes, but I've changed all the names and all the locations."

"Really, what's my name?"

"Rachel and you work at the Lenox Hill Hospital in downtown Manhattan."

"What's Jennifer's?

"Monica."

"Oh, and don't tell me, your name is Ross?"

"Ross? No way. Actually, I don't have a name. My name isn't mentioned at all, as the book is written in the first person."

"You've got this all worked out, haven't you?"

"With a little help from Google."

"But what about the sex?"

"Sex?"

"Yes, the sex we've had, and earlier?"

"Oh, the sex, yes, it's all in, every little detail, well, it will be, sex sells, look at Fifty Shades."

"I've never read that crap and stop fucking smiling."

"Sorry, I can't help it, it's the weed."

"And what happens to me in this bestselling book?"

"I haven't come to that part yet."

Lisa, nervously burst out laughing. "What do you mean, you haven't come to that part yet?"

"You won't die in it, don't worry."

"I won't die. Oh, thank you. Thank you very fucking much. Where's that joint?"

"Here you are."

She took another drag.

"This is crazy. This is fucking mad. I can't go to work. There's no way. I can't focus. I'm coming with you."

"What."

"I'm coming with you to meet Jennifer, Monica, whatever her bloody name is."

"It's Jennifer, and you can't, no way."

"Oh yes way. Oh yes, I'm coming. I'm involved big time. Her crazy stepdad wants to kill me, so I'm coming, end of story."

"No pun there then."

"Stop it. Just fucking stop it."

"So, you're still going be with me?"

"I have to be, I've no choice, otherwise I'll be looking over my shoulder for the rest of my bloody life."

"But, but what about the police?"

"What about them?"

"Aren't you gonna call them?"

"No. We have to sort this out."

"But, you. Miss prim and proper, a nurse and all that."

"We all have a dark side mister, and I value my life."

"But, I'm a murderer. I nice one at that though."

"If there is such a thing. And, I know. I must be mad."

"Join the club."

"You'd better message her."

"I'll do it tomorrow, like I told her."

"No, no you won't, you'll do it now. In fact, give me your phone."

"It's alright, I'll do it."

"Give me your fucking phone," she demanded.

"Okay, okay, take it easy. Here you go."

"Take it easy. Are you mad?"

"Okay, sorry, wrong choice of words."

"What time?"

"What?"

"What time did you say you'll meet her?"

"Oh, ah, say midday."

"Where?"

"Oh, the Tower of London. Apparently it's her favourite place."

"Oh great, we can do a bit of sightseeing whilst we're there then."

"If you like."

"I was being flippant."

"So was I. Anyway, in the book we meet in Central Park."

"Just had to be didn't it. Okay, text sent. I'd better message work."

Just then my phone pinged.

Hey, was just thinking of you, looking forward to seeing you J x

"Is that your phone?"

"Yes."

"From her?"

"Yes."

"That was quick, let me look."

"What?"

"Just give me the phone."

"Okay. Okay."

"Oh, thinking of you and a kiss. This gets better every second."

"It's not like that, honest."

"Honest!" she laughed. "Don't worry, I'll soon put her in her place."

"Don't be hard on her, she just buried her husband."

"Don't be hard on her, what about me? Her crazy stepdad wants to kill me."

"He won't, I'll make sure of that."

"But how can you?" she asked as she started to message the hospital.

Before I could respond, she continued,

"Hold on. Hold on a second. It's all starting to make sense now."

"What is?"

I knew where she was going with this.

"The gloves. The cut on your stomach."

"Yeah. Sorry about that."

"Oh, and please don't say that driving me to work had anything to do with it?"

"Actually, it did."

"I fucking knew it."

"Well, I had to get rid of the evidence and the bins at the hospital seemed the perfect place."

"So, what exactly did you get rid of at my place of work?"

"The gloves, a mac and duct tape."

"Jesus fucking Christ."

Lisa put her head in her hands trying to take everything in.

"So, tell me the gruesome details, or do I have to wait till I read the book, that's if I'm alive. So, no, no, tell me, tell me right now."

"You sure?"

"No but tell me anyway."

"Well, I smacked him on the head with the brick first and then stabbed him to finish him off."

"Of course. I heard about YOUR murder on the news. But his finger, they said he had one missing?"

"He did. Actually, it was his right thumb, I had to cut it off to gain access to his phone."

"God. This is so fucking sick."

"I know, but Mad Dog needed it to gain access to the phone."

"Mad Dog, who the bloody hell is Mad Dog?"

"Mad Dog Maddox. The guy who's threatening to kill you if I don't do what he says. The crazy fucking stepdad who paid me twenty grand."

"What's his name in the book?"

"Bulldog."

"It just had to be didn't it. So, where's the thumb now, don't tell me, it's here?"

"No, not anymore, but it was, in the drawer over there." I nodded towards it.

"My God. So, I've been sleeping with a murderer and with a dead man's thumb in the bedside table?"

"Yes, I'm afraid so."

"But what about the knife you killed him with, what did you do with that?"

"Well, you know the lunch you made yesterday!"

TO BE CONTINED…………

Coming soon in book two…..

CCTV

THE train was motionless.

Unlike my state of mind.

Lisa and I were on the Jubilee line, underground between St Johns Wood, and Baker Street, the former home of the fictional Sherlock Holmes, which was the next stop. I sincerely hoped a similarly astute detective wasn't on my case. We'd been stalled and waiting, along with a carriage full of commuters, for a couple of minutes. It was eleven-fifteen. Forty-five minutes until the arranged meeting at noon with Jennifer, at her favourite spot, the Tower of London.

Earlier, before we'd even stepped out of the flat, I'd already received three messages from Mad Dog Maddox, threatening to call the police and to kill Lisa if I didn't own up to his stepdaughter that I'd murdered his son-in-law.

Being underground, with no signal, gave me some respite from him.

Lisa, sat to my left, in tight faded blue jeans, a white T-shirt and a black leather jacket, had been up all night, chain smoking and pacing the flat. Understandably she was ever so slightly on edge since I'd informed her that her life was on the line. As the train started to move, an attractive young woman, blonde, mid-twenties, wearing a smart navy blue trouser suit, stood up and made her way over to the doors, leaving a Metro newspaper on her seat, which was directly opposite mine. I thought about picking the paper up to see if the story of my murder was still newsworthy. I decided against it. The morning news on the radio before we'd left the flat hadn't mentioned the killing either.

Had the investigation died down?

"You okay baby?" I asked Lisa.

"Am I okay? Really! Am I okay? What do you think?" The sarcasm was cutting.

"Well, I'm just peachy! I mean, I used a murder weapon for making my lunch the other day, I slept with a dead man's finger in the bedside table next to me, my boyfriend is a murderer, and now I'm on my way to meet the wife of the guy he murdered. Oh! And her stepfather wants to kill me. I've never been fucking better!"

Made in United States
North Haven, CT
22 June 2024

53932175R00107